TO BE
EQUALS IN
OUR OWN
COUNTRY

WOMEN'S SUFFRAGE AND THE STRUGGLE FOR DEMOCRACY
SERIES EDITOR: VERONICA STRONG-BOAG

The story of women's struggles and victories in the pursuit of political equality is not just a matter of the past: it has the value of informing current debate about the health of democracy in our country.

This series of short, insightful books presents a history of the vote, with vivid accounts of famous and unsung suffragists and overdue explanations of why some women were banned from the ballot box until the 1940s and 1960s. More than a celebration of women's achievements in the political realm, this series provides deeper understanding of Canadian society and politics, serving as a well-timed reminder never to take political rights for granted.

Books in the series:

One Hundred Years of Struggle: The History of Women and the Vote in Canada,
   by Joan Sangster

Ours by Every Law of Right and Justice: Women and the Vote in the Prairie Provinces, by Sarah Carter

A Great Revolutionary Wave: Women and the Vote in British Columbia,
   by Lara Campbell

Our Voices Must Be Heard: Women and the Vote in Ontario,
   by Tarah Brookfield

To Be Equals in Our Own Country: Women and the Vote in Quebec,
   by Denyse Baillargeon

We Shall Persist: Women and the Vote in the Atlantic Provinces,
   by Heidi MacDonald

Working Tirelessly for Change: Indigenous Women and the Vote in Canada,
   by Lianne Leddy

DENYSE BAILLARGEON

TO BE
EQUALS IN
OUR OWN
COUNTRY

Women and
the Vote in Quebec

TRANSLATED BY KÄTHE ROTH

UBCPress

VANCOUVER & TORONTO

© UBC Press 2019

All rights reserved. No part of this publication may be
reproduced, stored in a retrieval system, or transmitted, in any form
or by any means, without prior written permission of the publisher,
or, in Canada, in the case of photocopying or other reprographic
copying, a licence from Access Copyright, www.accesscopyright.ca.

28 27 26 25 24 23 22 21 20 19   5 4 3 2 1

Printed in Canada on FSC-certified ancient-forest-free paper
(100% post-consumer recycled) that is processed chlorine- and acid-free.

Library and Archives Canada Cataloguing in Publication

Title: Women's suffrage and the struggle for democracy /
series editor: Veronica Strong-Boag.

Names: Strong-Boag, Veronica, editor.

Description: Includes bibliographical references and indexes. |
Contents: Volume 3: To be equals in our own country : women and the vote
in Quebec / Denyse Baillargeon ; translated by Käthe Roth

Identifiers: Canadiana (print) 20179076094 | Canadiana (ebook) 20179076108 |
ISBN 9780774838733 (set ; hardcover) | ISBN 9780774838481 (v. 3 ; hardcover) |
ISBN 9780774838757 (set ; PDF) | ISBN 9780774838504 (v. 3 ; PDF) |
ISBN 9780774838764 (set ; EPUB) | ISBN 9780774838511 (v. 3 ; EPUB) |
ISBN 9780774838528 (v. 3 ; Kindle)

Subjects: LCSH: Women – Suffrage – Canada – History. | LCSH: Suffrage –
Canada – History. | LCSH: Women – Legal status, laws, etc. – Canada – History. |
LCSH: Women – Canada – Social conditions. | LCSH: Suffragists – Canada –
History. | LCSH: Voting – Canada – History.

Classification: LCC JL192 .W67 2018 | DDC 324.6/230971–dc23

Canadä

UBC Press gratefully acknowledges the financial support for our publishing
program of the Government of Canada (through the Canada Book Fund),
the Canada Council for the Arts, and the British Columbia Arts Council.

We acknowledge the financial support of the Government of Canada
through the National Translation Program for Book Publishing, an initiative
of the *Roadmap for Canada's Official Languages 2013–2018: Education,
Immigration, Communities,* for our translation activities.

UBC PRESS
The University of British Columbia
2029 West Mall
Vancouver, BC V6T 1Z2
www.ubcpress.ca

CONTENTS

ON 25 NOVEMBER 1935, Idola Saint-Jean, one of the most radical feminists of her time, wrote to Mrs. Hernance Roy, a supporter of women's suffrage: "When the history of suffrage is written, the role played by our politicians will cut a sad figure beside that of the women they insulted." As Saint-Jean suggests, members of the Quebec legislature – especially the French Canadians – were strongly opposed to women having the right to vote, and they were not afraid to express their opinions in a heavy-handed fashion. During the 1920s and 1930s, when suffrage was debated in the Legislative Assembly, politicians felt free to shout sexually charged insults at the women who demanded this fundamental right.

Suffrage was the centrepiece of the early-twentieth-century feminist movement, and achieving it took a lot longer in Quebec than elsewhere in North America. In Canada, the United States, and Great Britain, most women won the vote during or just after the First World War. In some Australian and American states, as well as in New Zealand, they were enfranchised long before the twentieth century. Quebec women, by contrast, could not cast a provincial ballot until 1940. Like their counterparts in France, Belgium, and Italy, Quebec suffragists waged a long, bitter campaign, and the fact that women of European descent had already obtained the vote in other parts of Canada played a role. Politicians, intellectuals, and French Canadian clergy resisted giving Quebec women the vote because its absence reinforced the cultural difference of Canada's only majority French-speaking, or francophone, province.

In fact, Quebec women had been the first in Canada to vote. Those who satisfied certain landownership conditions could vote from 1791 until 1849, when that right was taken away. The atypical

Political rights such as the right to vote have been considered human rights since the United Nations adopted the Universal Declaration of Human Rights in 1948. Article 21.1 states, "Everyone has the right to take part in the government of his country, directly or through freely chosen representatives."

path travelled by Quebec women – from frontrunners to last place – is the central theme of this book. As its title suggests, it tells the story of their struggle for political enfranchisement, but it also details the loss or gain of other rights – legal, social, and economic – that generally extend from suffrage. In other words, suffrage is not treated as an isolated question but as the fulcrum for a group of individual and collective rights that are associated with human rights today.

In 1948, when the United Nations declared that voting was a human right, it echoed arguments that Quebec suffragists had put forward in earlier decades. On 8 April 1936, in a speech broadcast on radio station CKAC, Idola Saint-Jean declared, "We want [women] to enjoy the freedom of being human." She felt that excluding them from political life denied them their humanity, pure and simple, and for two reasons. First, because they could not elect their representatives, they were relegated to an inferior civil status. Second, the absence of political rights led to other forms of exclusion and discrimination that prevented women from acting independently and preserving their dignity. In Saint-Jean's view, they needed the vote to eradicate inequalities between the sexes and to overcome male domination.

Thérèse Casgrain, no doubt the most influential Quebec suffragist of her day, agreed. In an 8 June 1934 broadcast, she stated,

"Women suffer living conditions that are imposed upon them by a society in which men dominate." She continued, "For women, the right to vote [is] the only logical means compatible with our political system to ensure them the sanction that they must have at their disposal to be recognized and to maintain their rights." Clearly, like Saint-Jean and many others, Casgrain felt that enfranchisement represented not only an end in itself but also a way to guarantee that women would enjoy all of their rights as citizens.

Surprisingly, though historians have discussed Quebec women's suffrage in numerous essays and in books on the history of women, feminism, citizenship, or parliamentarianism, it has never been given a book-length treatment. Catherine Cleverdon, an American historian, was the first to write about women and the vote in Canada. In her book *The Woman Suffrage Movement in Canada,* published in 1950, she offers a sweeping history of the suffrage movement and its associations, on a national scale and in the provinces. The book painted a portrait of key events and characters in broad strokes and provided an early framework from which to interpret them. Republished in the 1970s during an era of feminist resurgence, it inspired a generation of historians and helped build women's history into a distinct research field.

Cleverdon showed that Canadian women had engaged in difficult battles but that their struggles for the vote had been much more civil than those mounted by British and American women. Canadian suffragists, she argued, employed patience rather than force, persuasion rather than violent demonstrations or harassment tactics. The difference, she contended, stemmed from the conservatism of Canadian society and of the suffragists themselves, who encountered apathy and even opposition from the great majority of women. She remarked that if winning women's suffrage in Canada was generally "more a struggle than a fight," it was in Quebec that "the struggle came nearest to being a fight" – a reference to the irreconcilable positions of those for and against

The term "suffragette" is generally reserved for activists, mainly British, who were notable for their vigorous battles and even violent actions. Those who adopted less radical, more peaceful tactics were called suffragists.

suffrage, who continued to clash until the beginning of the Second World War.

Since Cleverdon's book first appeared, historians have tried to explain why Quebec women took so long to gain the vote. Two explanations stand out: conservativism in the province and the nationalist convictions of its male elite. However, neither male politicians nor the Catholic Church opposed enfranchisement on principle. Rather, civil and religious authorities took a stance based on what they stood to gain or lose in allowing women to vote. In France, the Catholic Church supported female suffrage because its leaders expected that women would vote against elected representatives who favoured secularism (the principle of separation of the state from religious institutions). Not surprisingly, the elected representatives themselves opposed women's suffrage for exactly the same reason. In Quebec, where the idea of strict neutrality of the state in religious matters did not exist, differences between politicians and the Catholic clergy were much less marked, at least on the question of women and the vote. Politicians and the clergy – both bastions of male power – consequently acted together to oppose female suffrage, which they believed could disrupt the sociopolitical order.

In other words, the fears of male elites lurked behind the antagonism to suffrage. In their opinion, it would cause French Canadian traditions – embodied in the figure of the mother who was completely absorbed in her household and children – to crumble, along with male domination. Given these fears, it's impossible to understand the struggle of Quebec suffragists without considering the "national question" and the roles that nationalists assigned to men and women to safeguard the nation. The experience of other countries, in the West and elsewhere in the world, offers good reason to take this dimension into account. Irish nationalists, for instance, opposed the female franchise because they believed it would undermine the traditional image of the Irish woman, which was integral to their movement. In both Ireland and Quebec, however, feminists and nationalists managed to overcome their differences over suffrage and form alliances because many early-twentieth-century feminists were as nationalistic as their male compatriots.

But did the bonds between French Canadian feminist and nationalist movements hamper the suffragist cause? When feminist historians tackled this question in the 1970s, they were rather harsh. Many advocated democracy and equality between the sexes, so they deplored that the suffragists had emerged exclusively from the bourgeoisie, or middle class. They denounced the suffragists' unconditional acceptance of woman's role in the family and their unquestioning allegiance to the Catholic Church. According to feminist historians, the francophone suffragists' attachment to family and religious values – two pillars of French Canadian national identity – led them to show diffidence, and even total submission, to the clergy, an attitude that undercut their demands for equality. This lack of radicalism may explain their failure to obtain the right to vote at the same time that other Canadian women did. However, radicalism or a high degree of activism didn't produce immediate results for suffragists in other countries, as the experience of the English suffragettes shows. Authors who have written about the thoughts and actions of the second generation of suffragists have been more sympathetic. As they have underlined, second-generation suffragists

such as Casgrain and Saint-Jean (who founded new suffrage organizations in the 1920s and kept fighting right up to the final
victory) were less nationalistic and more independent from the
clergy than earlier proponents of enfranchisement in Quebec.
Their approach was just as egalitarian and combative as that of
their English Canadian counterparts.

But exactly how determined, or even radical, were Canadian
suffragists? For feminist historians of the 1970s, demanding the
right to vote in the name of equality of the sexes would seem to
have been the only rationale worth rallying behind. In the 1990s
and 2000s, however, a new generation of historians throughout
the Western world demonstrated that many suffrage associations
and activists had invoked the *difference* between the sexes as a reason for enfranchisement. If permitted to vote, these women asserted, they could bestow their maternal qualities on society. The
predominance of this logic prompted historians to see it as an
ideology distinct from feminism, one known as maternalism. This
new perspective suggests that it was not exceptional for French
Canadian feminists to legitimize their demands for suffrage by
invoking the maternal nature of women. It could even be suggested that in emphasizing their maternal mission they were less
paralyzed by conservatism and more concerned with the idea of
empowering women. Moreover, in Quebec as elsewhere, suffragists employed both maternalist and egalitarian arguments, and
we can presume that some of those who used maternalist arguments did so not necessarily out of deep conviction but to reassure
a male audience particularly resistant to the idea of formal equality between men and women.

Maternalist arguments in favour of female suffrage also laid
siege to the idea of separate spheres for men and women, the
ideology that underpinned the patriarchal order. Born during
the French and American Revolutions, this ideology reserved the
public sphere for men and the private sphere for women, at least

in theory. Confined to the home, women would devote themselves to educating their children and caring for their households. In fact, this dichotomous vision of the respective roles and places of the sexes never kept women from circulating or acting in different ways in the public sphere. However, this view of gender roles had a significant impact on how nineteenth-century Western societies conceived the relationship between women and the political world. In fact, it was in the name of separate spheres that the right to vote was withdrawn from women in Lower Canada (later known as Quebec) during the nineteenth century. Without denying the centrality of the maternal and domestic role of women, those who employed maternalist arguments often insisted that the border between the two spheres was porous. The household, they stated, was not a cloistered space totally separated from the rest of society. In reality, the private sphere was influenced by the public sphere. Given this, why should women not, in turn, be able to influence the political world to make society better and thus protect their households? In other words, the maternalist conception of relations between the private and public spheres can be interpreted as a form of challenge to the patriarchal order – something that opponents to women's suffrage understood clearly.

The struggle for the vote involved the social action of elite women, who, after the turn of the twentieth century, formed groups and created charitable or reformist associations that coalesced into the women's movement and later came to be known as feminism. Their goal was to fight various social problems associated with industrialization, and they demanded the vote to better influence political powers and bring about social reform. Even if they could not vote, these elite women nevertheless saw themselves as citizens who had a right to participate in managing the affairs of state. Their involvement in the reform movement was a type of political activism. In this sense, the history of women's suffrage demands a broader conception of political history and citizenship, one that makes room for those who could not vote but who nonetheless intervened in the public sphere to transform society.

Women's social action helped pave the way to the vote and equality for women, but it also required suffragists and reformers to present themselves as models and educators to the working and immigrant classes that they claimed to aid. There were exceptions, but most leaders of the women's movement came from the middle class and shared its prejudices. They rarely took into account the priorities or needs of disadvantaged populations, on whom they simply wanted to impose their values. Some historians have even contended that bourgeois women in English Canada saw the vote not as a right for all women but as a means to increase their own moral influence over the poorer classes. This argument has been criticized for lacking nuance and for overemphasizing the conservatism of suffrage leaders. The fact remains, however, that most suffragists were privileged, and they managed to attract only a limited number of working-class and rural women to the cause. We know little about why these women shunned the right to vote, but we do know they were particularly numerous in Quebec and that their refusal is a fundamental aspect of the history of suffrage.

Research has also shed light on the eugenicist and even racist ideas of some English Canadian suffragists. The vast majority of them were white, and their maternalism caused many to view reproduction, both biological and social, as essential to strengthening what they considered the superior Anglo-Saxon race. This type of discourse, permeated with terrible prejudices, was stimulated by fears of race suicide or degeneration, which they believed would be brought on by declining birth rates among English Protestants and rising immigration rates among races that were deemed foreign and inferior. Some historians argue that the conservatism of the suffragist movement in Canada is explained, in large part, by its desire to be associated with the construction of a white, colonial society. English Canadian activists wanted to participate in the British imperial enterprise, and to do so, they were forced to present themselves in a respectable light – that is, as moderates.

Other studies have shown that suffragists throughout Canada did not share a uniform view of race: they conceived racial differences in varied ways that were not always hierarchical. We know little about attitudes in Quebec, but we do know that the black and Asian communities were very small in the first half of the twentieth century; in 1921, each community comprised about two thousand people, who lived mostly in Montreal. Consequently, the white population's fears of and animosity toward these communities were not expressed as virulently or in as organized a way in Quebec as they were in British Columbia and Nova Scotia, for example. Nevertheless, francophone activists did employ racist logic. For example, they cited as unfair the fact that women in "uncivilized" countries could vote, whereas they themselves could not. In addition, their lack of interest in the situation of Indigenous women, whom they never mentioned, constituted a form of unspoken racism.

Indigenous women did not participate in the suffrage movement. Nor did they gain the right to vote federally in Canada until the 1960s. But their struggle against various forms of violence and discrimination since that decade – that is, their political activism – stands alongside earlier demands for the franchise or legal equality for married women. Indigenous women battled for the abolition of provisions in the Indian Act that deprived them of their Indian status if they married white men and denied them the right to belong to their own communities (and all the privileges associated with them). The concept of intersectionality, which emphasizes the complexity of identity and the intermingling of various forms of discrimination, calls on us to consider Indigenous women's struggles as but one of many manifestations of the feminist fight for democracy.

This book is inspired by arguments and concepts such as maternalism developed by multiple generations of feminist historians and political scientists. I pay particular attention to the ideology of separate spheres and to the national question that coloured debates on women's suffrage until the mid-twentieth century because they are essential to understanding the resistance that Quebec suffragists faced, including from the many women who said that they did not want to vote. The refusal of these women to have a democratic right conferred upon them is essential to an overall portrait of the struggle for women's suffrage. In a similar vein, it is important to scrutinize all the arguments made by those pushing for suffrage, even the less glorious ones. To that end, and to capture the experiences of women in all their diversity, *To Be Equals in Our Own Country* spans more than two centuries, from 1791, when certain women in Lower Canada were granted the franchise, to today, when all women in Quebec can vote but many contend that it is not enough to ensure their full participation in liberal democracy.

TO BE EQUALS IN OUR OWN COUNTRY

Aren't these people exercising a dubious right –
a right that was claimed to belong to them and
on which the Chamber had never wanted to
make a decision?

– AUGUSTIN [AUSTIN] CUVILLIER,
LA MINERVE, 3 FEBRUARY 1834

The right to vote is not a natural right for either
men or women; it is granted by law. The only
questions to be answered are whether women
may in fact exercise this right to the benefit of
the state and whether they can exercise it with
good reason.

– PETITION BY PIERRE FAUCHER,
ROMAIN ROBITAILLE, AND ALL ELECTORS OF QUEBEC CITY,
3 DECEMBER 1828

ONE

PIONEERS OF SUFFRAGE

In this drawing of a nineteenth-century polling station in Lower Canada, two returning officers sit with their poll books, looking on as a voter prepares to take an oath. More voters, including a woman, wait their turn to cast their ballots. Female property owners could vote, as suffrage was linked to property. However, their inclusion in the electorate, due to an interpretation of the Constitutional Act of 1791, was increasingly being contested. At a time when women were associated with the roles of wife and mother, their presence in polling places was becoming unacceptable. Their right to vote was withdrawn in 1849.

THE INDIGENOUS PEOPLES who occupied the St. Lawrence Valley well before contact with Europeans had their own political organizations, in which women played roles of varying importance, depending on the nation. In Iroquoian societies, which included the Huron-Wendat and the Iroquois, they took an active part in decision making, notably with regard to the selection of chiefs. Clan identity and status were also handed down through women, who were held in great esteem and sometimes exercised real power in their communities. French and then British settlers decried the modes of government of these Indigenous nations and the status they granted to women. These were ignored when the colonists set up a parliamentary system in the late eighteenth century. There are large gaps in our knowledge about the political functioning of the eleven Indigenous nations that occupied the territory of Quebec – especially in northern and boreal communities, which had less contact with whites. Even so, it can be stated that the Indigenous peoples were excluded from the debates that led to parliamentary democracy, just as they were later excluded from the establishment of the Canadian nation-state.

A form of democratization may have existed in preindustrial Quebec at the beginning of the nineteenth century, but the notion of human rights did not emerge until much later. In this mainly rural society, the family – its perpetuation and prosperity – was much more important than individual freedom and accomplishment. But though everyone, both men and women, had to meet the demands of the family group, the patriarchy particularly constrained women's autonomy. According to the Custom of Paris, the legal system that ruled in Lower Canada until the Civil Code replaced it in 1866, women remained under the authority of their father until they married and then of their husband. Only widows and adult women who never married escaped this legal guardianship – though not their family obligations. In fact, this society depended enormously on the work of all women, even those who were not married, and it was in the family, whatever its level of wealth, that they laboured. They could not work in a profession or hold public office, positions that were few and far between at any rate.

Yet, in this rigidly hierarchical society, women were permitted to vote between 1791 and 1849 if they satisfied certain conditions. This "right" was actually more a privilege because it was based on property. Moreover, it was granted to women not through a real desire to include them but because the relevant legislation did not specify that voters had to be male. In fact, if it hadn't been for the provisions of the Custom of Paris regarding women's and widows' property ownership, very few women would have qualified as voters. And so, women could vote because the electoral statute adopted in 1791 did not take into account the matrimonial regime of Quebec, the only British colony in North America in which French civil law prevailed. At a time when the ideology of separate spheres was becoming predominant, female participation in the electoral game seemed incongruous, even abnormal, and it became obvious that women should be denied the vote. The new conception of the place of women, in which they were relegated to the household, also had an impact on other dimensions of their lives, as can be seen in the role that they played in the rebellions of 1837–38 and the debate around the dower.

THE CONSTITUTIONAL ACT OF 1791 AND
FEMALE SUFFRAGE

Parliamentarianism in Canada and Quebec goes back to 1791, when Britain passed the Constitutional Act, dividing the enormous Province of Quebec into two new colonies – Upper and Lower

Canada – which lay on either side of the Ottawa River. The westernmost colony, Upper Canada (now part of Ontario), would be subject to English common law. Lower Canada (now part of Quebec) was home to the vast majority of the white population of French descent and would remain under the Custom of Paris. Each colony had an elected Legislative Assembly whose prerogative was strictly limited. Although the assembly could pass laws, the executive branch, concentrated in the hands of the governor, a Legislative Council, and an Executive Council – formed mostly of British-born politicians – could block its decisions. In Lower Canada, the little latitude left to the assembly quickly poisoned relations between the French Canadian elites, who formed the majority of elected members, and the Crown representatives who sat on the two councils – a situation that led to the rebellions of 1837–38.

The limitations imposed on the assembly in 1791 were accompanied by a similarly restrictive view of the electorate. As was often the case in the early parliamentary democracies, the right to vote was not universal but was subject to property ownership. The thinkers of the time felt that only possession of property conferred the necessary economic independence, and therefore the independence of mind, to perform citizens' duties. People who did not own property had no material interest to defend and could thus be easily manipulated to vote according to the wishes of others. In other words, owning property indicated that an individual could freely express his (or her) political will. As a consequence, and as in England, the Constitutional Act conferred the vote on British subjects who were twenty-one or older and who either owned land or a building of a certain value or were tenants who paid a minimum annual rent. Significantly, the Constitutional Act referred to these voters only as "persons" and did not stipulate that they must be male. As a result, a number of female property owners became eligible to cast a ballot. Most who did so were widows, but some were single adult women or married women who owned property in their own right or who lived apart from their husbands. Their participation in the electoral system made Lower Canada unique in the annals of female suffrage in Canada.

In fact, even though the Constitutional Act of 1791 applied to both colonies, it seems that significant numbers of women exercised their right to vote only in Lower Canada. This situation flows from the fact that the Custom of Paris, which defined the property rights of married women and widows, was more generous than the common law. Although the Custom subjected a wife to the authority of her husband, it offered her certain economic guarantees. For instance, unlike the common law, which considered the husband the sole owner of the couple's assets, it recognized that wives could own real property, such as assets that they inherited. They were also entitled to half of the assets acquired by the couple after they married. Given the legal incapacity of married women, which prevented them from exercising rights or recourses under the law, their husbands managed all these assets for the duration of the union. When the husband died, however, the widow inherited half of the community property, which she could now administer on her own, just as she regained the capacity to manage her own assets. She also received a dower, which consisted of the income from half of her husband's real properties. This is why, in Lower Canada, a greater number of widows possessed chattels of sufficient value to give them access to suffrage. Also, by signing a marriage contract in front of a notary – a provision that did not exist in English law – a wife could become the legal owner of property and was thus qualified to vote. If she held the status of public merchant, which enabled her to manage her commercial affairs independently, she qualified as well. Although historians note that a few women did cast ballots in other British North American colonies, it is not surprising that the number of women who voted in Lower Canada was unequalled elsewhere. Nevertheless, exercising this right was often difficult and quite random, mainly because electoral procedures favoured discretionary practices. That is, individual jurisdictions could choose whether to allow women to vote.

According to the Constitutional Act of 1791, the vote had to be held at a site chosen by the riding returning officer, who, assisted by clerks, also supervised the election itself. Officers had to ensure that each voter's identity, profession, residence, and capacity, as well as the name of his (or her) preferred candidate, was properly recorded in the poll book provided for the purpose. The ballot was oral, not secret. Voters simply stated the name of their preferred candidate, which meant that everyone at the poll knew how they had voted. The candidates attended the process as well and could question the legitimacy of electors, requiring that they take an oath before the returning officer to prove their validity. If all the candidates agreed, they could prevent someone from voting. Elections sometimes lasted for days because the polls did not close until an hour had elapsed since the last voter cast a ballot. In 1832, a by-election in the riding of Montreal West dragged on for a record twenty-three days. Given that the candidates and their supporters could easily keep count of the votes received by each aspiring representative – information often published in the newspapers – obstruction tactics and even violence were common.

The surviving poll books give some indication as to how many women attempted to vote, who they were, how many were disqualified and why, and, for those who did manage to cast a ballot, which candidate they chose. Historian Nathalie Picard analyzed the poll books for the Montreal region between 1792 and 1849 and found that of the 961 women who went to the various polling stations over the period, 857 succeeded in voting. The vast majority of them (74 percent) were widows and single women.

Although the women who voted satisfied the property requirements, their level of wealth varied greatly, as revealed by the range of their professions (including day labourer, labourer, milliner, seamstress, and public merchant). It therefore cannot be said that only very wealthy women voted. About 60 percent were francophones, which means that 40 percent were from Britain or elsewhere. At the time, people of British descent constituted about 20 percent of Lower Canada's population, so anglophones were overrepresented among female electors. Nevertheless, they were outnumbered by the francophones, and 60 percent of ballots cast by women favoured the Parti canadien, or the Parti patriote that succeeded it in 1826 – the same proportion as that of all francophones who voted. Picard's research also shows that of the eighty-two women who voted in the 1824 election, thirty-two were Indigenous, most of them Mohawk widows living in Sault Saint-Louis (Kahnawake), Huntingdon County. They did so despite the objections of candidate Vincent Dufort, casting their ballots in favour of Austin Cuvillier and Jean-Moïse Raymond of the Parti canadien. We must remember that the colonial government had not yet formalized the system of Indian reserves to which, starting in the 1850s, First Nations men and women would be confined and deprived of their property rights, which excluded them from the electorate. According to Renaud Seguin, it was not unusual for Indigenous people from the St. Lawrence Valley to vote in the first half of the nineteenth century, as the proximity of their communities to colonial settlements encouraged them to avail themselves of a right that they saw white people exercising.

The available sources show that opposition to the women's vote began to grow in 1827. For instance, though eighty-six women voted in the riding of Montreal East in 1820, only one of the two women who presented themselves in 1827 succeeded in doing so, for the candidates opposed the other simply because she was female. As the poll book recorded, "Voter a woman.

Candidates agreed not to take female vote." Picard quotes an 1823 letter from Pierre Bédard, long-time Parti canadien leader, to party member John Neilson, in which Bédard stated that in Trois-Rivières, "women vote like men." This seems to imply that the practice was a settled matter. As Bédard explained, "It is only in cases in which women are married and the husbands are alive that they [the husbands] vote as heads of the family. When the husband does not own property and the woman does, she is the one who votes." Bedard's comment indicates his acceptance of the fact that linking suffrage with property would automatically empower some women to vote. In 1828, when Andrew Stewart was elected in the Upper Town of Quebec City, some voters expressed their dissatisfaction by sending a petition to the Legislative Assembly. In it, they mentioned that a widow's vote had been rejected during the contest, emphasizing the connection between political rights and the status of property owner. On 22 December 1828, the Patriote newspaper *La Minerve* printed the text of their petition, which stated that "property, and not people, is the basis for representation." The petition also invoked the intellectual equality of women and men, the fact that a woman sat on the throne, and the need for women to reconcile domestic and political responsibilities, as the two were intimately linked:

> The petitioners have not learned that there exists in the minds of women any imperfection that places them lower than men on the intellectual scale ... One might say that nature has formed women for domestic life; however, the English constitution allows a woman to sit on the throne ... In fact, it would be very impolitic and tyrannical to circumscribe her [a woman's] efforts and to say that she cannot feel the greatest interest in the fate of her country and the preservation of its rights.

The same day, the newspaper published another petition that contested the election results in the William-Henry (Sorel) riding because "girls, married women, and widows" had voted illegally – a claim refuted by Wolfred Nelson, the Parti patriote candidate who won the seat. In a request submitted to the assembly, Nelson pointed out that the Tory candidate, James Stuart, had "received the votes of many women, and had even sent to find one at Isle-aux-Noix at great expense, who, after taking the oath, voted although she was not qualified." Because six of the ten female electors had opted for Stuart, one might expect that his supporters would be the last to quibble about the women's vote. They brought it up not so much because they opposed female suffrage per se but because it was useful ammunition in their attempts to discredit Nelson. At least, this was implied in the various petitions, reproduced in *La Minerve,* that were inspired by the William-Henry results. In fact, unlike the Upper Town petition, which focused solely on female suffrage, the William-Henry petitions denounced the fraudulent use not only of the women's vote, but also of the men's vote – according to some, three brothers who voted had all claimed to own the same property. The petitioners also accused their adversaries of having used intimidation tactics or resorting to attempts at corruption. In short, these documents give a clear indication that women figured as one example among others of fraud or electoral misconduct, not as the primary target of indignation. Nevertheless, female voters were particularly likely to provoke controversy, providing a radical contrast with the rather serene acceptance of Pierre Bédard quoted above.

As far as one can judge, it seems that before 1832, members of the Parti patriote were favourable to the women's vote – as long as it helped propel their candidates to victory. In fact, before the 1830s, only the *Quebec Mercury,* a newspaper that supported the colonial administration, published a detailed argument against female suffrage, as illustrated in an August 1827 article. After suggesting that the vote of a married woman was fraudulent by definition because she owned no property – which was not always the case under the Custom of Paris – the writer maintained that women who voted would neglect their domestic duties, to the great misfortune of the nation. Furthermore, female suffrage would ultimately enable women to hold office, and the resulting sexual attraction among members would distract them from affairs of state and sow chaos in the Legislative Assembly. Also, female members could become pregnant at any time, which would prevent them from taking their seats. In the opinion of the *Quebec Mercury,* female attributes and roles were incompatible with the exercise of citizen rights, a stance that the Patriotes would soon embrace.

The 1832 by-election in Montreal West, in which a Tory named Stanley Bagg ran against Daniel Tracey of the Parti patriote, seems to have marked a turning point. In a bitterly contested race, Tracey won his seat by the slimmest of margins – only four votes – and the election itself was marred by violence. Two years later, in 1834, the Legislative Assembly passed its first statute to deprive women of the vote. As historian Bettina Bradbury shows in her essay "Women at the Hustings," the links between these two events, though they are very real, are more complex and less direct than they might initially seem.

Bradbury discovered that a large number of women, 225, wanted to vote in the Montreal West by-election. She also found that many of them, 60 percent, saw their qualifications as electors challenged, as opposed to a rate of 30 percent for all the elections that Picard examined. Clearly, the ability of women to vote was contested more strongly during this election, which took place at a time when the conflict between Patriotes and supporters of the colonial authorities was heating up. But it must be noted that the tightness of the race also drove each party to scrutinize the qualifications of everyone who intended to cast a ballot. Thus, the fact that women's votes were more frequently challenged during this election could be explained by the extreme closeness of the contest, not solely by the desire to exclude women. In fact, the partisan press, which followed events closely and reported the slightest incident, did not object to the presence of women at the polls, in and of itself. However, a 3 May article in *La Minerve* challenged the legitimacy of the "ladies" as electors by stating that, like "elderly voters and the infirm," they were the hapless pawns of both political parties. They were brought to the polling station at the last minute, and almost unwillingly, for the sole purpose of harming the rival candidate. In short, by linking female voters with other vulnerable people, the newspaper suggested that they were easy to manipulate and could not think independently, which helped to devalue and delegitimize their votes.

The women who voted were certainly more assertive than the Patriote newspaper implied, as they sometimes encountered staunch opposition from candidates and were thus required to publicly defend their rights. They were generally accused of sharing the political opinions of their male relatives or friends and of supporting the same candidates, but this is not surprising and does not prove that they were easy to influence. In fact, men who were related to each other or of the same ethnic or social origin behaved similarly. But what was acceptable, and even logical, for men seemed suspect when it came to women. This double standard fed the idea that only men could form authentic political convictions and claim the status of citizen. In this perspective, women's support became an extra argument for denigrating a rival candidate. He was so desperate that he had to count on their votes to win the election. This discourse was particularly pernicious not only because it defined the legitimate elector as male, but also because it demeaned the masculinity of those who courted the female vote. At the time of the 1832 election, no one was yet suggesting that women be excluded from suffrage, but the door seemed open to questioning a right that, as we recall, had never been officially conferred upon them.

According to some historians, the extreme violence of the 1832 election, which prefigured the rebellions of 1837–38, was instrumental in convincing politicians that, for their own safety, women had to be kept away from the polls. Other historians believe that the Patriotes were in the greatest hurry to disenfranchise women because female voters supported their adversaries, but this interpretation does not hold up. Although the Tory candidate did garner 105 female votes in the 1832 Montreal West election, against 93 for Tracey, Picard shows that women tended to favour the Parti patriote. Given this, one would expect the Patriotes to support the retention of the female franchise. But they did not, so we must look to other factors for an explanation, including, particularly, the influence of republican discourse on Patriote ideas about the place of women in society.

Like the French and American revolutionaries before them, the men who led the rebellions of 1837–38 deemed that citizenship status should be reserved for men. Its corollary, the defence of the common good, required a detachment from private concerns, which women, who reproduced and maintained life, could not achieve. Swayed by the ideas of thinkers such as Jean-Jacques Rousseau, the Patriotes felt that motherhood and the education of children should be women's first duties and main contribution to the nation, which attached them irrevocably to the private sphere. This role was seen as far from negligible, as it created future citizens, but it was complementary to that of men, who alone had the skills to conduct affairs of state because they alone could transcend family ties. What is more, women's participation in political life seemed unnatural because it denied their most profound inclination, which was to devote themselves to their families. In reality, men's political activity was entirely dependent on the domestic work of women, whose management of the household freed them to pursue their civic duties. Thus, it is hardly surprising that men insisted on keeping women at home. If society were to function properly, women had to fulfill the domestic role, so they could not leave home without threatening public order and the common good. This idea came to be associated with a new, more rigid socio-sexual order, sanctioned by the ideology of separate spheres. Women's confinement to the private sphere even became a sign of respectability. Venturing out in public was evidence of immodesty that bordered on indecency and could only encourage the corruption of morals, including political morals. Ontario historian Cecilia Morgan, who has studied the political and religious discourses of Upper Canada, observes that the language of politics assumed a definitively masculine connotation between 1791 and 1850. By contrast, religion and moral questions were debated in terms associated with femininity. These domains, as well as the gender identities that corresponded to them, were constructed in reference to each other.

The conception of citizenship as male, which became integral to bourgeois democracies in the nineteenth century, was forcefully voiced in early 1834 during the brief debate on the disenfranchisement of women that arose in the Legislative Assembly. Expressing the idea that female participation in citizen life was contrary to good morals, Louis-Joseph Papineau declared,

> As to women voting, that is something it is right to destroy. It is ridiculous, nay odious to see wives dragged to the hustings by their husbands, girls by their fathers, often against their wishes. The public interest, decency, the modesty of the sex demand that these scandals should not be repeated any more. A simple resolution of the Chamber would exclude such people from the right to vote.

Papineau's speech, often quoted, constitutes a sort of aberration, as few wives or girls could exercise the franchise, whether willingly or not. Thus, it was the very idea of seeing them at the polls that repelled him, due precisely to his Rousseauist ideas.

Although Papineau's words obviously conveyed his republican convictions with regard to the role of women and the separation of spheres, they do not explain why the assembly chose to disenfranchise women at precisely that moment. Some historians suggest that it wanted to bring Lower Canada's electoral law into line with that of Britain, which had excluded women since 1832, but this is not totally convincing. According to Bradbury, the investigation that followed the turbulent Montreal West by-election played a more immediate role.

The violence of that election, which ended with the death of three Patriote followers, prompted the assembly to look at all the events that surrounded it. In January 1833, during the hearings of the committee that handled this investigation, Jacques Viger, Papineau's cousin and the future mayor of Montreal, put female suffrage under the microscope. He supplied an exact tally of the women who voted for each party, according to their civil status, and a list of all the women who voted after the announcement that the poll would close if no elector arrived during the next hour. By his account, twenty-three women cast their ballots during this crucial period. Fifteen of them supported Stanley Bagg, the Tory candidate. This information strengthened the Patriote feeling that Bagg had unfairly recruited the female vote in a last-ditch effort to win the race. Viger specifically targeted Marie-Claire Perrault, the wife of assembly member Austin Cuvillier. Formerly of the Parti patriote, Cuvillier had recently crossed the floor to the government party and was thus *persona non grata* among the Patriotes. Viger revealed that, like her husband, Perrault had voted for the government candidate just before the poll closed. In fact, the 21 May edition of *La Minerve* had already challenged the validity of her vote. According to her marriage contract, she maintained separate ownership of her assets, but she had agreed to pay Cuvillier's debts, which the paper saw as paradoxical. If her assets truly were separate, she would not have had to help him in this way.

It was following this investigation that the electoral statute was amended to exclude women. As reported in *La Minerve* on 3 February 1834, assembly member John Neilson suggested that the act should be revised to settle "many doubtful questions," including "the right for women to vote, which is still undecided." Papineau's opinion, quoted above, was part of a long response to Neilson made a few days later. Considering Viger's revelations during the 1833 investigation, Papineau's statement seemed not only a reflection of his republican convictions linking citizenship and masculinity, but also a barb aimed at Austin Cuvillier due to his defection. In fact, only Cuvillier responded to Papineau, perhaps because he felt personally attacked. He did not, however, defend women's right to vote. Rather, he reproached Papineau for harping on the immodesty of female voters, given that he himself had "received their votes with pleasure." He also stated that women who voted were exercising "a dubious right – a right that was claimed to belong to them and on which the Chamber had never wanted to make a decision." In other words, though he denounced Papineau's reasoning, he arrived at a similar conclusion: it was not entirely legitimate for women to vote, as the assembly had never explicitly ruled on the question. Because no other member took part in this exchange, we can deduce that in the end, lawmakers on both sides of the floor agreed on the fundamental issue: women should no longer vote. Therefore, the 1834 statute stipulated, "As of and following the passage of this law, no girl, woman, or widow may vote in any election in any riding, city, or town in this province." It was adopted unanimously. It should be noted that in 1831, when Montreal was incorporated, only male Montrealers who owned property and were twenty-one or older had been given the right to vote. This too may have influenced the lawmakers' decision.

The 1834 statute was repealed in 1836. Although its demise had nothing to do with the question of the women's vote, it had disenfranchised them for two years, which had a definite impact on their voting behaviour thereafter. Barely more than a dozen women voted between 1836 and 1849, when the law was again revised and they were denied the vote for almost a century. By all evidence, the main goal of this revision was to standardize electoral procedures throughout the Province of Canada, which was created in 1840 when Upper and Lower Canada were merged after the rebellions. Catherine Cleverdon links the assembly's 1849 decision to deprive women of the vote to an 1848 meeting of American feminists at Seneca Falls, during which they demanded new rights, including the franchise. However, the Seneca Falls meeting had not yet achieved the legendary status that it later attained. The Canadian legislators may have known of it, but it is just as likely that their decision was a reaction to the 1848 Springtime of the People in Europe, which demanded the broadening of male suffrage and, more timidly, the instigation of female suffrage. The members of the Institut canadien, founded in 1844 by French Canadian intellectuals to promote republican ideals, were well informed of these struggles and supported their main objectives, including universal male suffrage. The move to disenfranchise women may also have been linked to the fact that some women had voted in Halton County, in the west of the Province of Canada, during the 1844 election. Due to their participation, the Tory Party won the seat by a mere four votes. The reformers who steered the electoral revisions of 1849 would have wanted to ensure that such a thing never occurred again.

At any rate, and quite remarkably, the decision to disenfranchise women was not preceded by major debates – either in 1834 or, even less, in 1849 – as if it were simply self-evident. As we have seen, only men commented on the question of female suffrage in the 1820s and 1830s, as if their opinions mirrored those of the

JULIE BRUNEAU PAPINEAU
(1795–1862)

The daughter of Pierre Bruneau, member of the Legislative Assembly of Lower Canada, and wife of Louis-Joseph Papineau, Julie Bruneau was known for her abundant correspondence with her renowned husband, who was often called away due to his political activities. A fervent supporter of the Patriote cause, she followed the debates in the assembly and the political negotiations, constantly asking him for news in her letters. She had nine children, including Azélie, who married Napoléon Bourassa, the painter, architect, and man of letters. Azélie was the mother of Henri, founder of the daily Le Devoir, ardent nationalist, and influential anti-feminist.

women in their families, and the women themselves had no need to speak in public. By the same token, women did not protest against the loss of the vote – neither in 1834 nor in 1849, collectively or individually. In fact, surviving correspondence and other writings by women of the time give no hint of indignation, or even unhappiness, about their exclusion from suffrage. Even Julie Bruneau, Papineau's wife, whose correspondence with her husband testifies to her passion for politics, did not comment on the subject, though she did not hesitate to disagree with him on other questions. As Mylène Bédard reports in her book *Écrire en temps d'insurrections,* she even reproached him in 1831 for requiring utter submissiveness from her despite his promotion of freedom and independence for people in political matters.

It would therefore seem that women shared the increasingly prominent ideology of separate spheres. After all, it did hold them in high regard, though only if they accepted its sexual division of roles and functions. This did not mean that they lost their interest in politics or that they withdrew entirely from the "civic, economic, and associative extensions of the public domain," as Marilyn Randall explains in *Les Femmes dans l'espace rebelle*. But it seems that they did not attach the same importance to suffrage as did the feminists of the early twentieth century. Furthermore, the republican and bourgeois vision of the place of women in society that was spreading during this period would have a major impact on female participation in the rebellions and on the protection of widows' economic rights, as we shall see.

WOMEN AND THE REBELLIONS

The exclusion of women from political citizenship did not stop the Patriotes from demanding their support during the rebellions against the British authorities in 1837 and 1838, as long as they stayed within the bounds of the domestic sphere. For instance, women were asked to boycott the British imports that generated taxes to fill state coffers. Referring to the American revolutionaries of the previous century, who had encouraged similar tactics, the Patriotes tried to rally women to this cause. "Let us examine what the Americans did, under similar circumstances," Papineau urged (as reported by Mylène Bédard). "Even the women ... were resolved to help their husbands, fathers, and brothers resist the horrible oppression that their tyrants were preparing for them ... I call upon the women of Canada; I beseech them to help me, to help us destroy this revenue, from which our oppressors forge chains for us and our children."

It was thus as consumers, and indirectly as producers, that women were asked to join the fight, with their domestic work compensating for purchases, particularly of fabrics and clothing.

The Patriotes went further: they called for the establishment of factories that would replace British goods and materials. A resolution adopted during a general assembly and reported in *Le Canadien* on 7 May 1837 stated "that we will consume by preference products manufactured in this country: that we will see as worthy of the motherland anyone who establishes factories for silk, blankets, fabrics." The Patriote newspapers show, however, that this production was mainly undertaken by women, and journalists always commented approvingly on people who wore "fabrics made in Canada" when they attended meetings and banquets. More than the women's work, what drew attention and seemed worthy of mention was the fact that both sexes proved their patriotism by dressing appropriately. As a *La Minerve* journalist wrote proudly on 28 September 1837, "The adoption of patriotic garments is spreading everywhere. The ladies cede no quarter to the gentlemen in their rejection of articles of foreign manufacture in their wardrobes."

The newspapers were even more complimentary when these ladies were married to political leaders. For instance, under the title "Honour to Our Patriotic Ladies," the 20 October 1837 edition of the *Vindicator,* an English-language Patriote paper, paid tribute to Émilie Hérigault, the wife of Toussaint Pelletier, and Adèle Berthelot, the wife of Louis-Hippolyte Lafontaine. They had been the first in Montreal to wear domestically made clothing:

> The patriotic ladies were noticed yesterday, *en promenade* with robes of étoffe du pays, of an exquisite and most fashionable *mode,* the appearance of which elicited the highest praise from all who saw them … When the ladies thus evince their determination to assist their brothers and husbands in the salvation of their country and in defence of their rights, the defeat of RUSSELL, GOSFORD, and DEBARTZCH is more than probable.

As this comment shows, wearing the right clothes became both symbol and measure of support for the Patriote cause. And when the wives of political leaders dressed patriotically, the gesture even seemed to guarantee victory. On 27 June of that year, the *Vindicator* had exhorted women to wear clothes made with Canadian fabrics and had linked the renunciation of imported clothes – costly, frivolous, and often indecent – with the reinforcement of feminine modesty and defence of the national cause. "Women of Canada!" it announced: "There is a demon destroying your country's prosperity, the virtue of your children and the happiness of your own hearth ... The demon that I speak of, that hath taken possession of, and sullied, the purity of your minds, *is an inordinate love of dress.*" In utterly republican logic, the excessive love of beautiful clothes became a danger to both women's virtue and the prosperity of the nation, understood from the moral and economic points of view. Because women's main responsibility was to educate future citizens, it was imperative that they preserve their modesty to provide a good example, which was to be conveyed by both their confinement to the home and their choice of simple, decent, locally made clothing.

The Patriotes also encouraged the creation of women's patriotic associations, and their newspapers mentioned their existence and activities with an enthusiasm that probably betrayed their rarity. In fact, only three or four associations were founded. Except for the Association des dames patriotiques du comté des Deux Montagnes, the first to be established, all were situated in the Richelieu Valley, the epicentre of the rebellions. In general, their meetings concentrated on celebrating the Patriote cause with banquets and, eventually, on adopting political resolutions, but essentially they simply supported the demands and strategies devised by men.

And so, on 23 August 1837, when the Association de Deux-Montagnes was founded, the Patriote newspaper *Le Canadien* reported that women in the riding "had launched a patriotic association for the purposes of acting, *in the sphere within which their sex is permitted to be active,* for the protection and defence of Canadian rights and liberties" (emphasis added). The paper noted that the women planned to hold another meeting, but it is not certain whether it took place. In Saint-Denis, according to the 28 September issue of *La Minerve,* Patriote women committed themselves to encouraging their men to support the cause "of the people and to take upon themselves all the sacrifices necessary for it to triumph." They also promised to encourage the development of local industries by using only fabrics made in the country and by refusing to purchase imported products. During a meeting in Saint-Antoine, which was intended simply to organize "a country dinner," as reported in *La Minerve* on 21 September, citizens saluted the women by discharging their guns. Inspired by their example, some of the women grabbed the weapons and shot them off, "with admirable poise and skill." On 25 September, *Le Canadien* quoted a woman who had been there: according to her, the female sharpshooters had wanted to "show that they would be capable as needed to handle firearms." In fact, women did not play a combat role during the rebellions, though they certainly sewed banners, melted spoons to make ammunition, concealed and cared for fugitives, and suffered the repression of the British Army and partisans who were loyal to the colonial power.

Ironically, the only two women who took up arms during the insurrection, and who were widely talked about in the press, supported the government forces. Their names were Hortense Globensky and Rosalie Cherrier. Even though their home villages mostly favoured the Patriote cause, they openly sided with the colonial authorities, being shunned by their communities as a result. Both were attacked by Patriotes who were outraged by their loyalty to the Crown, and both used their guns to defend themselves, their families, and their properties, not to fight in any

HORTENSE GLOBENSKY
(1804–73)

The descendant of a German surgeon who immigrated to Canada in 1776, Hortense Globensky was the wife of Guillaume Prévost and the sister of Frédéric-Eugène Globensky, who ran for the Tory Party in the 1834 election and whom she vigorously supported. In the summer of 1837, when the Patriotes attacked her house, she refused to leave it, which would have meant abandoning the body of her recently deceased child. Instead, she threatened her assailants with her husband's gun and succeeded in driving them off. This exploit earned her a silver teapot bearing the inscription "Presented to Madame G. Prévost, of Sainte-Scholastique, by several loyal persons of Montreal, in testimony to her heroism, greater than that expected of a woman, on the evening of 6 July 1837."

particular battle. Rosalie Cherrier, a cousin of Louis-Joseph Papineau, was also targeted due to her "dissolute" morals because she lived apart from her husband. In other words, the participation of these Loyalist women fell into the domestic sphere, just as it did for the Patriote ladies. The actions of all these women, Patriote or Loyalist, thus testifies to the politicization of the private sphere and, in the same breath, to the porosity of the borders between the private and the public, despite the claims to the contrary. In fact, although women were officially barred from public life, in the sense of citizen duties, the point of doing so was to nurture the blossoming of public life, according to the republicans – a clear illustration that the rhetoric around the private sphere was always political. In this view, the private was the very condition for the existence of the public.

In the same vein, women's actions during the rebellions were constantly justified by the legitimacy that their support brought to the revolutionaries – support that, in turn, verified the rightness of the cause. For the Constitutional Party, however, calling upon women as reinforcements simply revealed the weakness of the Patriote movement. Obviously, a party that was driven to "feminize" its adherents, and thus itself, had to be extremely feeble. Pro-government newspapers regularly ridiculed the Patriotes and minimized their importance by reporting that their meetings drew as many women and children as men. The Patriotes, meanwhile, often simply denied that women played any significant role in their meetings, showing a reluctance to place them on an equal footing with men. Although the leaders and supporters agreed that the role of women should be broadened to include involvement in the national struggle, they continued to support the ideology of separate spheres. For proof of that, we need look no farther than the Declaration of Independence of Lower Canada, proclaimed by Robert Nelson in March 1838. Unsurprisingly, it included only universal male suffrage, while it abolished the dower.

THE QUESTION OF THE DOWER
Although the Patriotes initially sought to defend the dower, their stance changed during the 1830s. The dower – the right of a widow to derive income from the property that her husband had owned when she married him or that he later inherited – existed in many areas in the early nineteenth century, but it could vary greatly from place to place. A product of the Custom of Paris, the dower in Lower Canada was more generous than in the other colonies of British North America, the United States, and England. In her essay "Debating Dower," historian Bettina Bradbury explains that in most common law regions, a widow's dower was composed

of the profits and rents drawn from one-third of her husband's assets – assets that would pass to the children when she herself died. However, the husband might convince her to renounce her dower, and thus her dower right was not inalienable. Under the Custom of Paris, the dower applied to half the property belonging to the husband at the time of the marriage or that he later inherited. This "customary" dower automatically applied and was inalienable unless the couple had signed a marriage contract before a notary in which the wife agreed to receive a stipulated dower – a specified amount of money – instead.

English merchants who settled in the colony objected to the customary dower because they saw it as hindering their freedom to make contracts. They particularly wanted to dispose of the provision of the custom under which the dower remained attached to the land, even if the husband decided to sell that land while he and his wife were living together. As women could not renounce the customary dower after they married, and the dower had precedence over all other creditors, it represented an appreciative protection for widows. However, it was a real conundrum for anyone who purchased land, as he might discover years later that a widow held rights to it. In the view of the British merchants, the customary dower was like a secret debt that hampered the sale of land and its accumulation for speculative purposes. Thus, they rose up against it and demanded the creation of dower-registration offices so that everyone could obtain reliable information on the obligations that encumbered landownership.

Until the mid-1830s, most francophone political leaders opposed the idea of registering dowers and felt that the customary dower proved the superiority of French law with regard to protection of widows and their children. Thereafter, however, their position resembled that of the English merchants. The Parti patriote, composed of professionals, landowners, and merchants in the process of consolidating their economic positions, also came to see the dower as seriously limiting the freedom of men to make land deals and as a barrier to capital investment and the establishment of industries in the colony. In a 1 February 1836 letter to *La Minerve,* the writer complained about the abandonment of a motion to amend the dower law. As he suggested, "The tacit imposition of the customary dower is, in our state of society, an evil that has already produced too many ruinous effects." He emphasized that the customary dower was no longer acceptable in a society in which "the frequency of property transfers ... makes these assets an object of business as quotidian as that of merchandise on shelves." He pointed out that because many men were ignorant of the marriage laws, one could hardly assert that a man who married without a contract deliberately chose to submit himself to the customary dower. "Therefore," he concluded, "in the husband's view, it would be only just and for the woman nothing unjust, if the legislature stopped this legal recourse to the hidden tax that is the customary dower."

Once the subject of deep discord between French Canadians and British, the customary dower was now unanimously opposed because its provisions, designed for a relatively stable peasant society, did not favour the free circulation and accumulation of capital typical of a society in which commercial exchanges were becoming the main source of wealth. However, the issue remained undecided at the dawn of the rebellions and was not addressed until after the defeat of the Patriotes. The Special Council that now managed the colony until a new assembly was elected finally imposed fundamental changes on the dower laws.

On the one hand, as Bradbury explains, the Special Council's ordinance required the registration of stipulated dowers – those included in marriage contracts – so that widows could benefit, in priority over any creditor, from the usufruct of properties that came to them from their husbands. The land to which the dower applied also had to be clearly identified. On the other hand, the ordinance gave women the right to consent to the alienation of the property on which their customary dower was supposed to be exercised, which meant that their legal incapacity was lifted in this particular case. In other words, married women received the dubious privilege of being able to renounce one of the few legal rights that they possessed. Finally, the council's ordinance also specified that the customary dower could be attached only to land that the husband owned at the time of his death. The council did not abolish customary dower, which would not occur until 1866, when the Civil Code was adopted. But it eliminated its inalienability by giving women the right to consent to the sale of land to which it applied. This amounted to extinguishing their rights on the land sold because the dower now applied only to land owned by their husbands at the moment of death. Widows' right to a dower – as well as the relations between husband and wife within the marriage – was thus reshaped to favour the development of an emerging capitalist economy.

⌘

Like the abolition of the female franchise, women's relatively marginal participation in the 1837–38 rebellions and the changes made to the dower testify, each in its own way, to the reconfiguration of gender relations during the first half of the nineteenth century. During this period, women were deprived of certain rights to facilitate the installation of a liberal capitalist society in which the bourgeoisie became the dominant class. In a society that had long been patriarchal, men – certain categories of wealthy ones, at least – appropriated the right to preside over the fate of the nation and to conduct its economic affairs while simultaneously consigning women to the home. Obviously, the public and private spheres were much more porous than the republican rhetoric admitted. The injunction that women should limit their field of action to the family was very far from strictly respected.

This was notably the case for elite women who engaged in charitable work during the early nineteenth century, an activity that would become the base from which they would eventually claim the right to vote. Nevertheless, the assimilation of women with domesticity and maternity would profoundly affect attitudes and would haunt the feminist movement when it claimed the right to vote. How could a woman be both mother and citizen? The English feminist author Mary Wollstonecraft had posed that question in the late eighteenth century. At the turn of the twentieth century, it remained unresolved.

If our vote as women is to have any value in the world at all it must be because it represents the distinctively feminine element in character and life. It is the difference between men and women that constitutes our claim. The more womanly "she" is the more she is needed, the more masculine the less!

– JULIA DRUMMOND, *LE COIN DU FEU*, JANUARY 1909

By participating in political struggles, women would forsake the role that nature has assigned them. They would desert their post as guardians of the cradle and, following false ambitions, they would renounce everything that has up to now been the charm and the breadth of their life: losing themselves for the happiness of those they love!

– MADELEINE HUGUENIN (ANNE-MARIE GLEASON),
LE JOURNAL DE FRANÇOISE, DECEMBER 1908

TWO

GIVING WOMEN
A VOICE

Believing that they could help resolve various social problems,
women began to campaign for the vote at the turn of the
twentieth century. This *Montreal Herald* cartoon of November 1913
exhorts a privileged woman to sacrifice a bit of her comfort to
join the fight against the exploitation of female workers and child
labour, among other scourges.

DURING THE LATE NINETEENTH century, the indifference – or, at least, the silence – that had greeted the 1849 abolishment of female suffrage would be replaced by a growing desire among some women to obtain the vote. The struggle began cautiously, however, as the influential ideology of separate spheres hindered a broad mobilization. Engaged in social and philanthropic works, middle-class women were the first to express a desire for a more active role in state affairs, but their political activism took various forms, and the demand for suffrage did not achieve prominence for some time. In the first decade of the twentieth century, the fight was concentrated mainly at the school board and municipal levels, where a few victories were won. Although some women hailed this as paving the way to the provincial and federal franchise, others hesitated to support a demand that they saw as excessive or inappropriate.

THE EMERGENCE OF THE WOMEN'S MOVEMENT
Before they began to call themselves feminists and demand the right to vote, the women who involved themselves in the public space during the 1880s and 1890s were active in a patchwork of associations that fed into what would soon be called the women's movement. Some groups, such as music and literary clubs, were intended to edify their members, but most focused on urban poverty. This was keeping pace with industrialization, which transformed social relations and inflicted hardship on numerous people, many of them women. The movement to found charitable organizations had visibility in some cities, notably Quebec City

and Sherbrooke, but was strongest in Montreal, Canada's manufacturing and financial epicentre. The contrast between the wealth of the business bourgeoisie, ensconced in the Golden Square Mile, and the destitution of the labouring classes, crowded into unhealthy neighbourhoods, inspired numerous initiatives aimed at eradicating poverty. As a result, Montreal women's associations of all sorts more than doubled, reaching several hundred between 1880 and 1900. In reality, elite women had engaged in charitable causes since the early nineteenth century, as such work had long been a social responsibility of the better-off, especially women, and a manifestation of their faith. As several feminist historians note, the religious dimension of charitable activity meant that organizations founded by lay people were generally identified with various Protestant denominations, Catholicism, and, toward the end of the century, Judaism. Many were parish-based. In the 1850s, French Canadian women began increasingly to take the veil, a phenomenon linked to the socio-economic upheavals of the period. This development was accompanied by a growth in the number of Catholic institutions that provided care for orphans, single mothers, the elderly, the sick, juvenile delinquents, and people with handicaps.

The burgeoning of women's charitable associations between 1880 and 1900 was thus anchored in a well-established tradition. However, the context in which it occurred transformed their orientation. For many years, elite women had been motivated by the idea of "doing charity," but now their volunteer engagement was increasingly grounded in what could be called a philanthropic perspective – the desire to attack the source of social problems by "scientific" means and ultimately to eradicate them. Influenced by the urban reform movement, which was also searching for solutions to the ills spawned by industrial capitalism, a number of women's groups advocated a rational approach to the problems engendered by poverty, such as housing and public health issues and behaviours deemed deviant (such as prostitution and

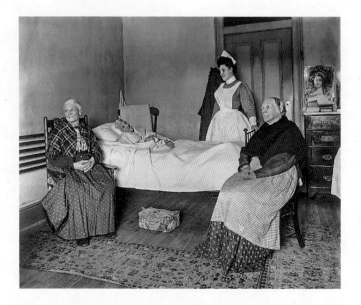

Founded in 1815, the Ladies Benevolent Society was the oldest Montreal laywomen's association whose purpose was to help the most vulnerable. Among the institutions that it founded was this refuge for elderly women. It still existed in the early twentieth century, when this photograph was taken.

juvenile delinquency). This new approach involved gaining better knowledge of these problems, greater co-ordination of efforts – financial and other – to fight them, and a more systematic application of the solutions proposed by experts. Prevention by educating the masses, rather than simply distributing assistance, became a key objective. At the same time, new causes, such as the exploitation of female workers, infant mortality, alcoholism (already denounced by male and mixed-gender temperance movements), and the moral dangers facing young women who came to the city to work, became the objects of attention.

The new view of women's social action that encouraged philanthropists to collaborate with reformists, including doctors, did not, however, exclude all religion. To the contrary: this fight against poverty found renewed justification in the Protestant Social Gospel movement and in the social doctrine of the Catholic Church, which, in the 1890s, advocated the Christian regeneration of industrialized societies through the elimination of their most flagrant inequalities. The new approach to social problems nevertheless led to a politicization of the debates regarding how to assist impoverished and marginalized populations. If it were to be effective, this aid had to be linked to transformations in social organization and to the adoption of government measures to implement them. Fighting against infant mortality, battling the proliferation of bars and taverns, and improving the lot of women who worked in factories required the state to intervene. It could mandate the pasteurization of milk, limit the number of liquor permits, and appoint female factory inspectors, to mention only a few examples. Appealing to government was then added to the arsenal of these philanthropists, whose objective had shifted from simply relieving misery via the occasional charitable gift to instituting reforms that would restore a certain level of social justice. They soon recognized that if they were to achieve this goal, they needed the vote. They also fought against the limitations imposed on them by their legal status and their restricted access to university education and the professions.

The volunteer activity of these women took on a new dimension during the 1890s, when a large number of associations gathered under the umbrella of the Montreal Local Council of Women (MLCW). Created in 1893, the MLCW was tied to the National Council of Women of Canada (NCWC), founded the same year by Lady Ishbel Aberdeen, the wife of the governor general. The NCWC was a branch of the International Council of Women (ICW), of which Aberdeen was the president.

Launched in 1888 by American feminists Elizabeth Cady Stanton and Susan B. Anthony, the ICW sought to unite women in Western countries in a sort of international parliament to give

LADY ISHBEL ABERDEEN
(1857–1939)

Born into an aristocratic Scottish family, Ishbel Marjoribanks married the Earl of Aberdeen and went to Canada with him when he was appointed governor general in 1893. President of the International Council of Women from 1893 to 1899 and from 1904 to 1936, she founded the National Council of Women of Canada, which aimed to bring together all women's organizations in the country. She was also the instigator of the Victorian Order of Nurses, a pan-Canadian philanthropic association that began in 1897 to offer home care to the sick and especially to poor pregnant women and their babies. A determined activist, reformer, and moderate suffragist, Ishbel Aberdeen was a notable figure of the women's movement Canada-wide and on the international level at the turn of the twentieth century.

them a stronger voice and make their actions more effective on both the national and global stages. (In fact, it was the ICW that encouraged the establishment of the NCWC, which was thus situated from the start in an international movement.) Female enfranchisement was the main goal of Cady Stanton and Anthony, but the forty-nine delegates from England, France, the United States, and India who attended the first ICW meeting did not reach unanimous agreement, and they had to fall back to objectives that were less controversial, such as promotion of women's status.

The mission of the MLCW, like that of other local councils in Canadian cities, was to encourage co-operation among its various member associations to improve their effectiveness, provide more force and visibility to women's social action, and enable them to exert greater influence in society. As Julia Parker Drummond, the first president, noted in 1894 (quoted by Elizabeth Kirkland in her dissertation "Mothering Citizens"), the MLCW intended to assist in the struggle against injustice and to promote measures aimed at the common good. She associated this with women's new awareness of their inclusion in the body politic:

> For in the power of our union we shall be able to make a determined stand against any injustice or wrong that may be brought to our observation, and to aid effectually in its redress; we shall be ready to promote, as far as possible, measures for the general good of all. *For we begin to realize that we women, too, are citizens,* and ... we are resolved to bear our part in the regeneration of our cities as we have never done before; and as a society we may sometimes have to fill that part by acting as a stimulus to the civic or public conscience. (emphasis added)

Thus, without yet having the right to vote, and before they even demanded it, the members of the MLCW appropriated the status of citizen to legitimize their actions in the public sphere. Obviously, their definition of citizenship went far beyond simply exercising democratic rights. It included the sense of belonging to a community that desperately needed their intervention if it were to function better. It was through their civic responsibilities that they envisaged their involvement in politics. As good citizens, they were obliged to inform the government of the problems of the hour.

As several feminist historians note, just as the concept of citizenship includes many realities that go beyond simply voting or having political rights, the concept of politics must also be broadened to include the extra-parliamentary and extra-partisan activities of those who cannot vote or take a seat in the legislature. In

GRACE JULIA PARKER DRUMMOND
(1861–1942)

The wife of industrialist George Alexander Drummond, president of the Bank of Montreal and a senator, Grace Julia Parker was the first MLCW president, a position she held until 1899. She also co-founded the Montreal section of the Victorian Order of Nurses and was a member of the Advisory Council of the Montreal Parks and Playgrounds Association, which called for the creation of children's playgrounds in working-class neighbourhoods. From 1911 to 1919, she led the Charity Organization of Montreal, which she had founded with her husband. During the First World War, she was involved with the Red Cross in England and with the Imperial Order Daughters of the Empire.

fact, though they did not have the vote, the elite women who led the MLCW and its member groups knew how to obtain support, whether financial or political, from the powerful men in their social circle. Through their new organization, which gave them the weight of numbers, they threw themselves into an in-depth study of social problems, sometimes consulting experts. They prepared briefs for submission to government, circulated petitions demanding the adoption of laws or various measures, corresponded with politicians, requested meetings with the most influential ministers and even the premier, and sent press releases and articles to newspapers to publicize their activities. Although the electoral game was barred to them, some tools of public intervention lay within their grasp and were often wielded very effectively. For

Among francophones, nuns were often responsible for seeing to
the poor and the sick. In some cases, they worked with lay people
to operate health care institutions. For instance, Hôpital Sainte-
Justine pour enfants, founded in 1907 by a group of wealthy
French Canadian women, appealed to the Filles de la Sagesse
religious order to provide nursing services for the children. At
the time, the hospital was still housed in a private residence,
on De Lorimier Avenue, in Montreal.

example, the MLCW played a fundamental role in the adoption of
the federal and provincial laws covering juvenile delinquents in
1908. The nuns who administered health care and assistance institutions lobbied similarly, as their establishments required support not only from the church but also from the government,
which provided some of their funding.

And so, it cannot be said that the workings of power were
a mystery to MLCW leaders. As the close relatives of influential
men, they understood how business and politics worked, and they
knew how to convince their male kin to open doors for them.
Nevertheless, involvement in the public space was a minefield
into which women had to venture carefully. When the need was
desperate, their domestic responsibilities could extend to the

most vulnerable in society, itself considered a big family, but otherwise the ideology of separate spheres had restricted them to the home since the early nineteenth century. Attempting to directly influence public affairs by demanding reforms might easily be seen as flouting gender roles, and the founders of the MLCW were keenly aware of this. Kirkland reports that at its first annual general meeting, in 1894, Lady Aberdeen justified these interventions by emphasizing that they were grounded in the innate maternal qualities of women. "How can we best describe this woman's mission in a word?" she asked. "Can we not best describe it as 'mothering' in one sense or another? We are not [all] called to be the mothers of little children but every woman is called on to 'mother' in some way or another." And so, by claiming the title of mother, real or virtual, and presenting their "mission" as "mothering" society, the founders of the first women's movement sought acceptance for their incursions into the public sphere.

As briefly mentioned in the introduction, many feminist historians term this rhetoric "maternalist." Because it was based on the idea that biological differences between men and women could legitimize social action by women, maternalists sometimes disagreed with feminists, who demanded rights, notably the franchise, in the name of a shared humanity that conferred the same fundamental rights upon both sexes. This contrast sometimes hid important nuances. Although some maternalists firmly opposed women's suffrage because they differentiated between male and female roles, others saw it as necessary for the advancement of their cause. The conviction that the vote was indispensable to obtaining reforms thus brought maternalists and "equal rights" feminists together. At the close of the nineteenth century, when motherhood seemed the inescapable fate of married women, it was certainly very difficult to ignore this reality and advocate absolute equality between the sexes. Instead, most people who were active in the women's movement endorsed the idea of complementarity between the sexes. This did not imply any form of hierarchy or infer that women were inferior to men. On the contrary, many felt that women were morally superior to men. Nevertheless, the discourses of the difference between the sexes and of separate spheres probably helped to dissuade some women from demanding the vote. In fact, though the MLCW leaders did recognize that the success of their demands depended on a degree of political activism and easily reconciled their identities of mother and political actor working behind the scenes, it would take more time for them to link their philanthropic responsibilities with their rights as citizens.

A WOMEN'S MOVEMENT DIVIDED

At first, the MLCW was intended to be neutral in terms of religion. However, Charles-Édouard Fabre, the archbishop of Montreal, would not permit Catholic associations to join it. This applied to women's religious communities, many of which were employed in the health care and assistance sector. Also excluded were lay-women's associations steered by the clergy, such as devotional and charity groups that worked in the parishes. This restriction enraged Joséphine Marchand-Dandurand. "Religious questions have absolutely nothing to do with the program of the National Council of Women," she wrote in Le coin du feu, a magazine she had launched in early 1893. In fact, a few French Canadian women did manage to join the MLCW because it accepted individual memberships as well as group ones.

Marchand-Dandurand's indignation changed nothing. In 1896, among the thirty-two organizations that joined the MLCW, only one, the Association des dames patronnesses de l'Hôpital Notre-Dame, became an affiliate. Notre-Dame hospital had been established by French Canadian doctors, not by a women's religious community, as many were, so its ladies' auxiliary enjoyed a degree of independence from the clergy. Their founder and president, Marguerite Lamothe Thibaudeau, whose husband co-owned the Montreal Cotton Company, was also one of the few French

JOSÉPHINE MARCHAND-DANDURAND
(1861–1925)

The daughter of Félix-Gabriel Marchand, premier of Quebec from 1897 to 1900, Joséphine Marchand was the wife of Raoul Dandurand, a lawyer and senator who would be appointed Canadian representative to the Society of Nations. Raised in a liberal milieu, she published articles in various newspapers as a young woman and then founded her own magazine, Le coin du feu, *which ran from 1893 to 1896. Thereafter, she contributed to a number of publications directed by women, such as* Le Journal de Françoise, *established by Robertine Barry in 1902, and* La Revue Moderne, *created by Anne-Marie Gleason in 1919. Several times, she was vice-president of the Montreal Local Council of Women (1895–96, 1900–01, and 1906–07) and a member of its presidential office (1903–07). She was also provincial vice-president of the National Council of Women of Canada (1912–13 and 1917–19) and a co-founder of the women's section of the Association Saint-Jean-Baptiste de Montréal (1902). In 1907, this group gave rise to the Fédération nationale Saint-Jean-Baptiste. She was part of the delegation that represented Canadian women at the Paris World Fair in 1900 and the founder of* L'Oeuvre des livres gratuits *(1898), which distributed books to teachers in remote regions and to the poor.*

Canadian women to brave clerical opposition in joining the MLCW. She became its vice-president before being replaced the following year by Marchand-Dandurand. In that year, Katherine Samuel DeSola, an Orthodox Jew, and Eliza McIntosh Reid, a Unitarian, were also added to the executive council, making it truly ecumenical. Lady Lacoste (Marie-Louise Globensky), wife of Sir Alexandre Lacoste, senator and chief justice of the Quebec Court of Queen's Bench, also served as a vice-president when the MLCW was founded. Her daughter, Marie Lacoste Gérin-Lajoie, who became a dominant figure in French Canadian feminist circles during the early twentieth century, also held various positions in the MLCW, notably in its presidential office. Another major figure in the French Canadian women's movement, Caroline Dessaulles-Béïque, the wife of a financier, was also a member.

The ethnic and religious diversity of the MLCW encouraged its members to tolerate each other's spiritual sensitivities. For instance, meetings began with a minute of silence rather than a prayer. In the eyes of the Catholic Church, however, this precaution was not sufficient to guarantee the faith of its followers. It distrusted every initiative that the MLCW undertook, even such activities as organizing infant hygiene classes for French Canadian mothers, whose children were dying in great numbers. This attitude was not unique, as some evangelical Protestant women's groups, such as the Woman's Christian Temperance Union and the Young Women's Christian Association, also hesitated to affiliate with the MLCW, as their members found it difficult to work alongside adherents of other Christian denominations.

The clergy's reticence with regard to the MLCW, combined with rising tension between English and French Canadians and the articulation of Catholic feminist thought in France, finally ended the alliance between francophone and anglophone bourgeois women. Although they belonged to similar classes, and their social and political relations brought them together and enabled them to work for a time within a single organization, their divergent ethnic origins and religious convictions ended up being obstacles. This was especially true for the French Canadian MLCW members. Clearly in the minority, they felt towed along by their colleagues, who could easily impose their views.

The obvious solution was for the francophone women to create an organization of their own. The groundwork for this was laid in 1902, when the patronesses of the Association Saint-Jean-Baptiste de Montréal (ASJBM) obtained legal autonomy for their committee, a fundraising body whose purpose was to help pay the debt for construction of the Monument national, a French Canadian cultural centre. Formed of the wives of ASJBM administrators and those who agreed to pay an annual contribution, this now independent committee brought together most of the women associated with early French Canadian feminism in Montreal.

MARIE LACOSTE GÉRIN-LAJOIE
(1867–1945)

Marie was the daughter of Lady Lacoste (Marie-Louise Globensky), who was well-known for her charity work, and Sir Alexandre Lacoste, lawyer, judge, professor, and politician in the Conservative orbit. She became the most important French Canadian feminist of the early twentieth century. The family ambience seems to have encouraged social and political involvement. In fact, two of her sisters also became recognized public figures – Justine Lacoste-Beaubien co-founded Hôpital Sainte-Justine, which she ran for almost sixty years, and Thaïs Lacoste-Frémont was a journalist, public speaker, and women's rights activist. Marie married Henri Gérin-Lajoie, a lawyer, with whom she had four children. The oldest, Marie, founded the Institut Notre-Dame du Bon-Conseil, a religious community devoted to social action. Her grandson Paul became the first Quebec minister of education, in 1964.

Among them were Lacoste Gérin-Lajoie, Marchand-Dandurand, and Dessaulles-Béïque, who was president until 1913. There were also several journalists (Robertine Barry, Anne-Marie Gleason, Georgina Bélanger, and Éva Circé-Côté) who were already playing an important role in disseminating new ideas about women, their place in society, and female education. In winter 1904, Lacoste Gérin-Lajoie told a few members of the committee about her idea to transform it into an organization like the MLCW, a plan that was finally completed in 1907. The former association of ASJBM patronesses then became the Fédération nationale

Introduced to charity by her mother, whom she accompanied on her benevolent outings, Marie Lacoste also studied her father's law books, which acquainted her with the inferior legal status of married women. It was for them that she published, in 1902, a treatise on customary law that highlighted their legal limitations. In 1893, she joined the MLCW and directed its legislative committee, among other functions. She cofounded the Comité des dames patronnesses of the Association Saint-Jean-Baptiste de Montréal and then the Fédération nationale Saint-Jean-Baptiste, of which she was president from 1913 to 1933. She also created its publication, La bonne parole. *She campaigned for the right to vote at the municipal, provincial, and federal levels and involved herself in all the feminist struggles of her era. She fought for the creation of the first classical college for girls, which opened in 1908; for women's access to the professions, notably the law; for a minimum wage for women; and for reform of the Civil Code.*

Saint-Jean-Baptiste (FNSJB). Because the new group accepted only French Canadian – and therefore Catholic – charities as affiliate members, it received the cautious support of the clergy, which permitted women's religious communities to join it. These communities ran most French Canadian charity works, and they initially comprised more than half of the FNSJB's affiliated associations, which greatly strengthened it.

The fact that Catholic nuns were joining the new federation was testimony to the persuasiveness of Lacoste Gérin-Lajoie, who, having discovered the Christian feminism advocated by French feminists such as Marie Maugeret, set out to convince the clergy that it was perfectly compatible with Catholicism. The Catholic social action promoted by Pope Leo XIII reinforced her conviction that feminism was entirely honourable because it was a "work of justice and humanity," as she wrote to Maugeret in a letter quoted by her biographer, Anne-Marie Sicotte. In Lacoste Gérin-Lajoie's view, feminism was a question of defending human rights – on condition, of course, that it was a Christian feminism. In the request that she sent to Paul Bruchési, archbishop of Montreal since 1897, to obtain his support for the creation of the FNSJB, she specified,

> We want to unite French-Canadian women within a national association through the bond of charity so that they will help each other in life; and through the strength that unity gives, they fortify, raise, and develop women's action in the family and in society; working also for the prosperity of the country and the glory of God over all things.

Presented in these terms, also as reported by Sicotte, the project could not fail to win approval from Bruchési. However, his response shows that as the struggle for suffrage in Britain was becoming increasingly violent, he was not easily convinced of the inoffensiveness of feminism. "I can do nothing but approve," he said. "This is the *true* feminism, that which responds to the needs of our times and from which society can draw the greatest advantages. It is very different from that *other* feminism, which, on the pretext of claiming unknown rights for women, forgets the role that Providence has assigned to them in the world" (emphasis added). In essence, Bruchési repeated this message at the FNSJB founding congress in May 1907, during which he made a speech. "As the word 'feminism' has been introduced into our language, I accept it," he stated, "but I demand for it a Christian meaning, and I ask permission to define it this way: woman's zeal for all noble causes that Providence has assigned to her." He continued,

> It is not in your assemblies that we will hear talk of women's emancipation, and of her unknown rights ... responsibilities, public functions, and professions to which she should be admitted on the same footing as men; no, no, you will leave these declamations and utopias to others and you will seek simply to join forces to do good, in the field that is appropriate for you.

Bruchési thus imposed the limits within which the FNSJB was to confine its activities if it wished to win the sanction of the Catholic high authorities. At the time, their endorsement was essential to the success of any French Canadian initiative. The FNSJB would concentrate on charitable work, which appealed to related feminine qualities of devotion, compassion, and self-sacrifice associated with the domestic sphere. In the June issue of her magazine *Le Journal de Françoise*, Robertine Barry, who had also attended the inaugural congress, voiced her disagreement with Bruchési. She stated that "feminism would be wrong if it kept its favours only for housewives." Emphasizing that many women were not housewives and that having a home did not necessarily protect them from hunger and the cold, she asserted that "good feminism" must offer "all protection first and foremost" to them.

In other words, Barry, herself an unmarried journalist, felt that many women were forced to earn their own living, which should also be a concern of feminism. However, virtually no one else publicly criticized Bruchési's stance. In fact, most FNSJB founders, including Caroline Dessaulles-Béïque, shared the church's view. A 27 May 1907 report in *La Patrie* quoted Dessaulles-Béïque, who said that the FNSJB would not champion the "revolutionary feminism that has the goal of distancing women from their role and their home." It would opt instead for the "Christian feminism that has the goal of charity and duty. We do not want to deserve the rebuke received by women who step outside their sphere." In fact, however, the FNSJB leaders would often link the private and public spheres in such a way that women's political action would work in tandem with their social action – a tendency that the religious authorities, obviously, did not always approve.

It is worth noting that the beliefs of the FNSJB founders regarding the feminine sphere of action did not differ fundamentally from those of the MLCW. It too felt that women should be attached to the home and should spread their influence from its centre. Nevertheless, for these organizations, which continued to co-operate well after the FNSJB was founded, the acceptance of separate spheres did not preclude women from attempting to fulfill their mission by actively seeking more rights. For example, Lacoste Gérin-Lajoie worked for many years to have the Civil Code amended. However, she did not advocate taking away men's status as head of the family or obtaining perfect equality between husband and wife. At most, she wanted the abolishment of certain provisions that kept married women under marital guardianship, to the detriment of their maternal responsibilities. Therefore, the changes that she demanded were tied to the obligations of motherhood. The FNSJB and the MLCW also crusaded for girls' access to higher education and for women's suffrage, invoking maternalist arguments as their justification.

EARLY STRUGGLES FOR THE VOTE

In Quebec, the first women's suffrage campaign focused on municipal and school board elections. These early battles, which have received too little attention, reveal the importance that the women's movement attached to these levels of government. After all, they administered education, public health, and social assistance, which were key concerns for women. Given its vigorous calls for reform in these areas, the movement was drawn to local democracy, whose decisions affected the daily life of ordinary people – including mothers. Thus, it is not surprising that it concentrated on women's representation at this level.

Back in 1831, when Montreal was granted its first charter, women had been left out of its municipal electorate. In 1887, more than fifty years after men had been enfranchised, widows and single women who owned enough real estate to qualify obtained the right to vote in its civic elections – though not to run for office. Except for Quebec City, which also had a charter and which enfranchised these same categories of women in 1876, the cities and towns in the province were subject to the municipal code. In their case, an 1888 statute granted the vote to widows and single property-owning women; in 1892, this right was extended to widows and single women who were tenants. In 1899, the franchise was extended to female Montreal tenants who paid taxes, including water tax; men had enjoyed this right since 1860. At this point, married women, who were deemed incompetent under the law, were still excluded from voting in municipal and school board elections, even though some – those who were married with separation as to property – could have qualified as voters. The 1892 statute also permitted female property owners to vote in school board elections. In Montreal and Quebec City, however, school commissioners were appointed, not elected.

In 1897, when it learned that a seat was being vacated on the Protestant Board of School Commissioners, the MLCW tried to have a woman appointed to the position. Because the law that governed the school systems in the two largest cities of Quebec did not specifically exclude women from these seats, and because women were traditionally associated with education, the MLCW believed that it had every chance of obtaining the commissioners' approval. Perhaps intending to nip this plan in the bud, the commissioner who had announced his retirement changed his mind. The MLCW nonetheless pursued its campaign for a female appointee but failed to win the support of the Protestant school board authorities. Although they admitted that the law did not ban female appointees, they noted that no woman had yet held the position. Before this could occur, they insisted, the education statute must be amended. As it turned out, the Legislative Assembly did amend the statute, but not in a way that pleased the MLCW. It barred women from appointment as school commissioners, a disqualification that would be lifted only in 1942.

In 1902, at the instigation of Lacoste Gérin-Lajoie, the MLCW fought another political battle – this time, to stop Montreal from disenfranchising female tenants. The genesis of this was a recommendation from a reformist councillor that the municipal franchise be extended to separated women. This measure would prevent electoral fraud, as, in his opinion, estranged husbands often voted in their place. At the time, a special commission was reviewing the municipal charter, and when the MLCW supported the councillor's suggestion, it was forced to endorse it. However, it also proposed that female tenants should lose the right to vote, as very few exercised it, which simply encouraged fraudulent tactics. In this scenario, 4,800 tenants would be disenfranchised, whereas only a handful of women would be added to the 2,800 who remained.

And so, a struggle began for female tenants to retain the vote, while preserving that of women property owners who were separated from their husbands. This time, the MLCW, represented by Lacoste Gérin-Lajoie, who directed the entire operation, launched a press campaign to expose the ignominy of the measure. It pointed out the absurdity of attempting to combat fraud, usually perpetrated by men, by disenfranchising the majority of female voters. "A unique logic," Lacoste Gérin-Lajoie wrote ironically in a December 1902 issue of *Le Journal de Françoise*, "that punishes not the thief but the one who is robbed." In a letter to the mayor and aldermen, the MLCW asked them to abandon their planned amendment because it was unfair. As Elizabeth Kirkland reports, the letter stated, "We may safely assure that, in future, women will value their electoral franchise more highly, and will use it conscientiously for the common good, on account of the greater knowledge they will have acquired from the discussion of this question, and from the light thrown upon it by the press."

Unlike the demand to appoint a female school board commissioner, this one was widely publicized and focused mainly on the injustice of excluding taxpaying women from the voting booth. No doubt for this reason, the MLCW triumphed. Not only would women who were separated from their husbands now be able to vote, but female tenants who paid taxes retained their right to do so. As it had promised, when the new municipal election got under way in early 1904, the MLCW launched a fresh crusade, this time to convince women to vote, a right that they might well have lost. The campaign took the form of a large pre-election meeting that was held only in English, but at which it was proposed to produce a bilingual pamphlet asking women to cast their ballots in large numbers. *La Patrie*, which gave the meeting front-page coverage in its 22 January issue, interviewed a number of well-known people on the subject, both men and women. Every interviewee insisted that female suffrage was legitimate because all taxpayers must be able to vote. Many added that women should vote in local elections because municipal affairs concerned them specifically. According to this article, opinions on the question seemed to have reached consensus. Whereas one alderman feared the female franchise because women tended to support "the handsomest boys," some male interviewees stated that women were often better informed than their husbands on municipal affairs, as they were more directly affected by them. In short, no interviewee expressed animosity about the women's vote, which shows that tax-based women's suffrage was accepted unanimously. Apparently, even Archbishop Bruchési approved of women's participation in these elections, notably because Lacoste Gérin-Lajoie convinced him that anglophones might unduly influence municipal politics if francophones did not vote. His stunningly conciliatory attitude foreshadowed the position of the clergy in Trois-Rivières. In the early 1920s, they asked that women be able to vote in a referendum regarding the adoption of daylight saving time. The local church was hostile toward daylight saving time, feeling that it contravened the natural order established by God, and it counted on women to vote against the proposition, which was duly defeated. Obviously, clerical opposition to women's suffrage, which could be fierce, as we shall see, could sometimes be modulated if the issue at hand were imperative enough.

The articles published in various dailies during the week preceding the 2 February 1904 election tried to convince women that voting was in their interest because the policies and regulations that shaped their daily life were adopted at the municipal level. These covered the safety of drinking water, the cleanliness of streets and markets, the installation of public lighting, availability of parks and playgrounds, and tramway circulation. Also, and perhaps even more interestingly, many asserted that women had a rightful place at the polls, though apparently not everyone agreed. "A poll is a public place, it is true, but an eminently respectable site," insisted a short item in La Presse on 30 January. Three days earlier, La Patrie had opined, "We know that there may be some prejudices among our female readers: they have been made to believe that it is improper to exercise their citizenship right." Therefore, more than a half-century after the rebellions, the idea that a polling station was not a proper place for a woman seems to have persisted – or, at least, the bourgeois women who organized this press campaign thought it had. No doubt, the electoral mores of the time helped to reinforce this impression, as candidates commonly handed out profuse quantities of money and alcohol to sway voters to their side. According to some, the women's vote was even "regenerative," as *Le Canada* suggested on 30 January. Thus, once women had overcome their "instinctive repugnance" to go to the polls, as expressed in *La Presse* on 1 February, their natural dignity would return a certain lustre to the exercise of democracy.

According to Lacoste Gérin-Lajoie, women flocked to the polls on voting day – a success that inspired her to declare, as reported by Sicotte, "The ice is broken; I believe we will not backslide!" She was even more optimistic because her meeting with Archbishop Bruchési just before the election convinced her that women had almost won the battle for the vote. "I believe that we have made a big step toward suffrage and that the clergy is quite well disposed toward it," she wrote in her diary. Events would, of course, prove this optimism unfounded.

For the moment, the MLCW and the newly created FNSJB became involved, with no further opposition, in the 1909 referendum on the reform of the city's political structures, as well as in the municipal elections of 1910 and 1912. In 1909, with corruption endemic among municipal office holders, Premier Lomer Gouin both established a commission of inquiry and ordered that a referendum be held on the creation of a four-person control bureau to oversee the councillors' work. At the request of a citizen committee that had denounced the situation, the MLCW became involved in the melee by encouraging qualified women to vote in favour of the referendum. It passed by more than 80 percent, thanks in part to the women's vote. In 1910, during a municipal election that was to select members of a first bureau of control as well as aldermen, the citizens' committee once again asked for women's support to elect an honest team that would clean up the city. The MLCW, the FNSJB, and other women's associations pooled their resources to achieve this goal. They ensured that all eligible women appeared on the electoral lists, provided them with information that would inspire them to vote for reformist candidates, had them transported to the polls on election day, and kept track of those who did vote. The 1 February election was a landslide win for the reformist candidates. The next day, *La Patrie* acknowledged that "the female vote was an important factor in this success." Other newspapers agreed.

In fact, all the papers noted that record numbers had gone to the polls, which slowed the election process. This discouraged many who had to wait outside, in the cold, before getting their turn to vote. *La Patrie* attributed much of the delay to the inexperience of female voters. Many were unfamiliar with the procedure, so it had to be explained to them. Others were required to swear an oath to prove their eligibility – solid evidence of success by the women's organizations. The paper also reported on a delaying tactic staged by one disgruntled voter. Believing that the many women queueing behind him would favour the reformist candidate, whom he did not support, he deliberately dawdled while casting his ballot. Disheartened by the long wait, several women gave up and went home. Whether true or false, this anecdote shows that women were certainly not perceived as a negligible factor in this election, as their reputation for moral rectitude naturally positioned them on the side of candidates who were considered the most honest.

The positive experience of the 1910 and 1912 municipal elections, in which the MLCW and the FNSJB played similar roles, encouraged them to focus on obtaining female suffrage at the federal, and then provincial, level. However, the issues were quite different. Municipal suffrage was directly related to the status of taxpayer, if not of property owner, but this was not necessarily the case at the federal and provincial levels. In the early twentieth century, even if a minimal electoral franchise still existed in Quebec, most people felt that voting for the federal and provincial governments was thus not associated with the property owner who had a say because he paid taxes, but with the individual citizen. Women had difficulty embodying this generic individual, which meant that their struggle for suffrage now ran into fiercer opposition, including from many women.

THE WOMEN'S VOTE IN PUBLIC OPINION

In 1909, when the MLCW decided to demand the female franchise for federal and provincial elections, opinions were still strongly unfavourable to this step. The negative reactions of some MLCW affiliates proved how unpopular the idea was among women, as did some surveys conducted by newspapers during the 1890s and 1900s. The distribution of these surveys over time also reveals that the reasons for opposition did not change much. In December 1893, Marchand-Dandurand's magazine, *Le coin du feu*, asked fourteen well-known francophones – eight men and six women – for their opinions about expanding the franchise. Only two were in favour. Ironically, both were men: politician and journalist J. Israël Tarte and P.A.J. Voyer, editor of *Le Monde*. Even so, Tarte's agreement was only partial. His view was that the widened franchise should apply only to women "who do not enjoy the very respectable advantage of being under the power of a husband." Poet Louis Fréchette, who expressed himself in verse; the intellectual Arthur Buies; Jules Helbronner, journalist and labour activist; and Honoré Beaugrand, founder of *La Patrie* and former mayor of Montreal, all of whom belonged to liberal circles, declared themselves against women's suffrage. As reasons, they cited the roughness of political play, the weight of such a responsibility, and the importance of women's role in the family.

Most of the women whom *Le coin du feu* interviewed gave similar reasons. Writer Félicité Angers (Laure Conan) and Mary Louise King, wife of former premier Joseph-Adolphe Chapleau, felt that the franchise would only "corrupt" women and destroy their dignity. "Why would we want to throw ourselves into the political furnace," asked Mrs. Chapleau, "from which we might leave burned to a cinder or, at the very least, blackened?" In fact, this small survey signalled that almost all these people took a very dim view of the political world. The corruption, rudeness, and even violence that seemed to characterize the rather "virile" electoral habits of the time were seen as completely antithetical to women's "natural" delicacy, restraint, and honesty. Therefore, becoming involved with politics could only demean them. "For the love of heaven, do not diminish women to the point of making them voters or legislative members," exclaimed Arthur Buies. Marchand-Dandurand herself hesitated to take an unqualified stance. On the one hand, she "estimated that the freest [women] are [those] who have their affairs seen to by men," although in the "matter of education, especially primary school, mothers of families would make excellent legislators."

Fifteen years later, in late 1908, Robertine Barry, a former *La Patrie* columnist who had founded *Le Journal de Françoise* in 1902, invited her readers to send in their opinions on the question. More than sixty women – journalists, writers, teachers, and the wives of politicians and judges – responded. Their letters were published in the December 1908 and January 1909 issues of the magazine. Only thirteen were wholeheartedly in favour of suffrage, including three from the seven anglophones who replied. Some fifteen others expressed divided opinions, and thirty-three – more than half – were unequivocally against.

Like the 1893 survey published in *Le coin du feu*, this one was obviously not scientific, as it gathered only the views of women who wanted to commit their thoughts to paper. Furthermore, all were associated with the political, legal, or intellectual elite of Quebec. It is also impossible to know how many women declined to express their opinion, perhaps because they supported the demand for suffrage but feared to say so publicly. Nevertheless, the exercise was very informative, because it conveyed the feelings of women who were the most likely to influence public attitudes. Although they were not representative of the population as a whole, particularly its female members, one may presume that their variety of views reflected public opinion in Quebec society. Among those who opposed suffrage, many invoked the argument of separate spheres. "It is better to leave national politics to men and family politics to women," said the wife of the president of the provincial bar. Several letters pointed out that women already had enough responsibilities, without adding more. Only one or two stated flatly that possessing the vote was not "compatible with the highest ideals of womanhood," but at least six expressed uneasiness with seeing women lose "their charm" or referred to the "apparent weakness" that brought them masculine attention and protection. Overall, however, these women did not claim to be uninterested in political issues. On the contrary, some, such as the wife of Eugène Tarte, felt the need to stay informed on questions of public interest. "We are citizens, and the fate of our country should not leave us indifferent," she noted. But for her, as for many others, the biological differences between men and women, and the fact that women were mothers, necessarily led to a difference in functions. In her opinion, rather than exercising the franchise, women should "awaken public virtues and love of our country in men's souls" – a typically republican argument. Marie-Louise Sénécal, the wife of Conservative MP Frederick D. Monk, went so far as to say that women must "direct men's votes" by using their influence in the couple and the family. These women thus adhered to the ideology of separate spheres but without necessarily renouncing all form of political engagement or considering themselves non-citizens.

The belief that wives owed complete loyalty to their husbands also worked against suffrage. According to this logic, a female voter who differed from her husband as to choice of candidate would find herself in an untenable position. Voting to suit herself would amount to betraying her husband and was likely to trigger household quarrels. Respecting her marriage vow of obedience by voting like her husband would amount to betraying herself and would trample upon one of the great principles of democracy – the right to vote for the candidate of one's choice. People who invoked this conundrum ignored the fact that a woman could resolve it simply by keeping silent about which candidate she favoured. They also overlooked the prospect that husband and wife might agree on which candidate was best, no doubt because admitting these possibilities would weaken their argument. Nonetheless, their idea caught on well. In fact, though some women accepted that widows and single women should vote, as they did at the municipal level, they opposed the enfranchisement of married women, in order to avoid conjugal arguments. For them, suffrage seemed incompatible not so much with femininity as with conjugality. Men – the heads of the family – were supposed to represent the couple's will, as the French tradition brought to light by historian Anne Vergus would have it. Catherine Cleverdon similarly advanced the idea that Quebec society, more centred on the family than on the individual, was more open than English Canada to denying women the vote because they were supposedly represented by the head of the household. Behind these opinions also stood the certainty that married women would necessarily be influenced by their husbands and could therefore not vote in complete independence, an idea that had largely contributed to abolishing women's suffrage in the nineteenth century. Although some felt that only "free" women, as they put it, should vote, others believed that only "intelligent" or "educated" ones should enjoy this right. They did not mention what they thought of the fact that all men voted, regardless of whether they were intelligent or educated. Adine Taschereau, the wife of future premier Louis-Alexandre Taschereau, who was known for his fierce opposition to the enfranchisement of women, believed that it "would be an excellent thing" if they voted. "Why is half of the human race *and not the less good [half]* excluded from this privilege?" she asked (emphasis added). However, she did not feel that women should run for office, a view in which she was not alone. Some women opposed enfranchisement because they saw it as the inevitable precursor to the right to compete in elections – a development they could not condone.

Interestingly, women who favoured the franchise rarely resorted to maternalist logic. Instead, they referred to equality between the sexes and thus to the need to treat men and women on the same footing. For example, writing under her pseudonym Colombine, journalist Éva Circé-Côté stated, "Objecting to women's right to vote is to take us back to the shadowy ages when it was seriously wondered whether they had a soul. Defending their expressing an opinion is to defend their having one." Some proponents of suffrage invoked the moral superiority of women, a claim that tied into ideas about sexual difference. Most, however, asserted that women should have a say in choosing the men who governed them, because now, "they are engaged in all enterprises" and also because many questions debated in the Legislative Assembly transcended the separation of spheres. Marie Beaupré, a *Le Canada* columnist who wrote under the name Hélène Dumont, best expressed the absurdity of denying women the vote on the pretext that affairs of state did not concern them: "As if the laws – as a consequence, those whom our vote sends to make those laws in parliament – did not rule the family, marriage, education!" Obviously targeting claims about the difference between the sexes, Ethel Hurlbatt, principal of Royal Victoria College, a women's college affiliated with McGill University and founded in 1899, stated, "If women are different from men, representative government without them is incompleted representation of the State. If women are the same as men they presumably have the same need to vote as men."

The 1908 survey conducted by *Le Journal de Françoise* coincided with the intensification of suffrage demands all over the Western world, which no doubt explains the magazine's interest. In the early 1910s, as British suffragettes launched a shocking campaign of civil disobedience, smashing windows and pouring acid into letter boxes, other publications also held similar surveys. In October 1912, the *Montreal Star* sent reporters to various city neighbourhoods and to Westmount (a wealthy anglophone suburb) to find out how women, both francophone and anglophone, felt about enfranchisement. Pierre Chemartin and Louis Pelletier report that more than 50 percent of the interviewees, both anglophone and francophone, said that they were indifferent. Eighty percent of those who were not indifferent strongly opposed suffrage because they felt that "women are women and men are men, each with their own work to do." They also denounced the attitude of the British suffragettes as "the rabid and empty vaporings [sic] of hysterical women" and described their movement as "foolish," "disgraceful," "crazy," "rubbish," "silly," "ridiculous," and "outrageous." Their comments resembled those gathered during another survey, this one conducted by columnist Madeleine (Anne-Marie Gleason) and published in *La Patrie* in August and September 1913. In terms that were sometimes extremely violent, the women who responded, more than fifty of them, were practically unanimous in condemning the suffragettes. The mildest criticism was that their tactics were counter-productive. "I am an ardent friend of women's suffrage," wrote one, "but if I were an English judge I would burn at the stake all of these maniacs who dishonour a good cause." These correspondents, who typically remained anonymous, referred to the suffragettes as "fanatics," "hysterical women," "criminals," and "crazy women in petticoats who want to wear pants." Clearly, suffrage was such a hot topic that dungeons, the gallows, or the stake could be cited as just punishment for the suffragettes, whose behaviour was as unnatural as it was illegal. In total, of the fifty or so letters published, fewer than twenty favoured the enfranchisement of women. Once again, it is difficult to attribute a scientific value to the opinions gathered by the

Montreal Star and *La Patrie*. Nor is it possible to dismiss the idea that some of the letters received by *La Patrie* were penned by men. Nevertheless, they indicate that suffrage was having difficulty gaining traction. The women who wrote these letters, often outraged, obviously placed great weight on the role that society asked them to play. The ideology of separate spheres was their ultimate reference in assessing whether enfranchisement served their interests. On the whole, they felt that it did not. To them, earning a right that had intangible effects but could jeopardize their honour, dignity, and respect seemed little more than a fool's bargain.

⌘

The women's movement that first formed in the late nineteenth century in Montreal, as elsewhere in the Western world, aimed mainly to relieve social misery more successfully than simple charity allowed. Despite everything, the social action deployed by its adherents proved a main catalyst for suffragism. As its leaders gained political experience and status, they learned that being excluded from the electorate limited their effectiveness. Without access to the ballot box, they found it difficult to influence elected officials and force them to enact essential measures. Initially centred on schools and the municipal scene, the fight to obtain the franchise was therefore displaced, starting in the 1910s, toward the provincial and federal levels. In Quebec, this struggle spanned several decades because of formidable opposition, mainly by nationalist leaders and the clergy. In fact, as we shall see in the next two chapters, this opposition would intensify to the point that the only francophone province in Canada became the sole province that did not allow women to vote – proof, in the opinion of nationalists, of the superiority of French culture and the greater consideration that they accorded to women.

Although nature does not strictly forbid society from conceding to women the right to participate, through their franchise, in political elections, it clearly and strongly advises, except in light of a greater good, that they not be granted this right … The greatness of woman … depends neither on the right to vote nor on ineligibility … Each of the two sexes has the superiority of its gender and each of the two retains its superiority as long as it remains in its domain and fulfills its duties.

— PETITION AGAINST WOMEN'S ENFRANCHISEMENT, FEBRUARY 1922

THREE

BROADENING THE STRUGGLE

Les Suffragettes à Montréal

A l'Emmanuel Church, mardi dernier, une femme a revendiqué le suffrage féminin. Voyez-là plutôt criaillant ses plaintes aux compagnes en culotte.

DÉRIDEZ-VOUS TOUTES LES SEMAINES EN LISANT NOS HISTORIETTES COMIQUES ET INÉDITES.

To the amusement of her listeners, a smug (and mannish) suffragist informs the crowd, "Yes, ladies, we mustn't be afraid to show our supremacy." The text at the bottom of the image leaves no room for doubt as to the cartoonist's point: "At the Emmanuel Church last Tuesday, a woman demanded female suffrage. Look at her, in trousers, screeching her grievances to the companions."

When women began to demand the vote, condemnation was swift. To denigrate their claims, many cartoonists endowed the suffragists with masculine features. By depicting them as failed men, they implied that they had launched the battle for suffrage because they were unable to satisfy the opposite sex. The goal of this ridicule was to discredit both them and their claims.

DURING THE 1910S, the struggle for women's suffrage in Quebec heated up at the federal, then the provincial, level. Until the late 1920s, two enfranchisement groups successively occupied centre stage. These were the Montreal Suffrage Association (MSA), an anglophone organization founded in 1913, and the Comité provincial pour le suffrage féminin/Provincial Franchise Committee (CPSF/PFC), a bilingual body created in late 1921. After the majority of Canadian women obtained the federal franchise in 1917 and 1918, the MSA had attained its main goal and was dismantled, leaving the field free for the CPSF/PFC. Seeking the provincial franchise, it made its first appeals to Quebec premier Louis-Alexandre Taschereau in February 1922 but suffered a stinging defeat. This, combined with the hardening position of the Quebec Catholic Church on the issue, prompted it to lapse into dormancy until 1926. Given that women could now vote at the national level in American, British, and Canadian elections, and that most Canadian provinces had granted them the provincial franchise, one might expect that Quebec would follow suit. It did not. In fact, as in France, Belgium, and Italy, the campaign for suffrage would be long and arduous, and victory would not be achieved until the advent of the Second World War.

THE MONTREAL SUFFRAGE ASSOCIATION

In Canada as a whole, Ontario pioneered the fight for female suffrage, as women such as anti-slavery activist Mary Ann Shadd Cary began to demand the vote even before the first organization

CARRIE MATILDA DERICK
(1862–1941)

The first woman to be appointed as a professor in a Canadian university, Carrie Derick taught botany and genetics at McGill University until she retired in 1929. During her studies, after she was hired as director of practice assignments in McGill's biology department, and then following her appointment as a full professor in 1912, Derick encountered diverse forms of sex discrimination. No doubt, this experience spurred her to become one of the most fervent feminists of her time. A pioneer of eugenics, she wrote a vast study on mental deficiency, which she presented to the MLCW. She was also openly in favour of contraception – then illegal – which was seen as scandalous in certain circles. During her time as its president (1907–11), the MLCW adopted a resolution supporting women's suffrage, organized an exhibition on the issue, and invited English suffragettes to come and give speeches in Montreal. Derick also founded the Montreal Suffrage Association.

devoted to the cause, the Toronto Women's Literary Club, was founded in the 1870s. In Quebec, the MSA, created in 1913 and led throughout its existence by Carrie Matilda Derick, was the first group to make suffrage its sole priority. The Montreal Local Council of Women (MLCW), with which the MSA was affiliated and of which it was in fact the creation, had endorsed the principle of suffrage back in 1909. It was one of the first Canadian local councils to take a position on the issue, one year before the National Council of Women of Canada (NCWC) declared its support. After several years of social action and appeals to the public authorities for various reforms, the members of both organizations finally concluded that, like access to university studies and the liberal professions, the vote was an indispensable tool in the pursuit of their objectives. It must also be said that as male suffrage was becoming generalized due to the constant diminution of the electoral qualification (the amount of tax one had to pay to be eligible to vote), the exclusion of women increasingly stood out as a flagrant injustice.

The long decades between the 1877 creation of the Toronto Women's Literary Club, the first Canadian association to demand female enfranchisement, and the adoption of pro-suffrage resolutions by the NCWC and MLCW provide ample evidence that support for the cause was far from unanimous. In fact, the women's movement was strongly divided on the issue. In Montreal, the decision by the MLCW to come out in favour sparked opposition even within its own ranks, notably by Orthodox Jewish women, who firmly believed that a woman's place was in the family. "The Jewish woman believes in her home, her husband, her children and her religion. She is not a suffragist," stated Clara Holzmark Wolf in the *Jewish Times,* as historian Elizabeth Kirkland reports. According to Kirkland, it is very likely that Katie Samuel DeSola, who had sat on the MLCW executive since its inception, resigned from the organization because she disagreed with its pro-suffrage stance. Nor had the FNSJB yet signalled that it wanted to officially support the measure. However, in an October 1913 article published in her magazine *La bonne parole,* Marie Lacoste Gérin-Lajoie, now FNSJB president, wondered, "You know how quickly this idea [women's suffrage] is spreading around the world. Will our country escape the present evolution? It would be foolhardy to say that it will. That is why it is good to think about what role our national association will play under the impetus of coming events."

As Lacoste Gérin-Lajoie observed, the question of suffrage was on everyone's lips, as the urban guerrilla tactics and violence of the suffragettes had been making headlines for several years. In the United States, the struggle for suffrage on the national scale, already more than fifty years old, was intensifying as Alice Paul became a main strategist of the movement, pushing for adoption of the nineteenth amendment to the Constitution, which would give women the vote. In France, suffragists and suffragettes were attempting to put the women's vote on the agenda of the Assemblée nationale, without great success. And then there were the efforts in the other Canadian provinces and on the federal scene. In fact, the creation of the MSA alone was proof that Quebec was not immune to such questions. For the moment, however, it was mainly anglophones who were determined to seek the answers.

The MSA was founded due to the MLCW's desire to keep public interest focused on the women's vote, especially in English Montreal, by continuing the initiatives that it had launched. In 1909, when it officially pronounced itself in favour of enfranchisement, the MLCW began to invite women to give public speeches about the issue. Among the speakers was the famous English suffragette Emmeline Pankhurst. Her December 1911 stay in Montreal apparently inspired the decision to create the MSA. In February 1913, shortly before the official opening of the MSA, the MLCW organized an exhibition devoted to women's suffrage, as a way to prepare the ground for the new organization. For the next two weeks, visitors could attend debates, get their fill of documentation, purchase buttons and other souvenirs, listen to speeches given by women from England, the United States, and English Canada, and, especially, sign a petition supporting suffrage. Except for the *Montreal Herald,* which ran a number of relatively sympathetic articles on the event, it seems to have garnered little media coverage. On 2 February 1913, the editorial page of *La Presse* included a short commentary that took no position on suffrage but did say that the exhibition had been set up "tastefully." It praised Canadian feminists for being "more peaceful" than the English suffragettes: "Neither sulphuric acid, nor vitriol, nor any other corrosive is used as an agent of persuasion; the appeal is to reason, pure and simple." In other words, *La Presse* approved the exhibition not due to the merits of suffrage, but for the good behaviour of the women who promoted it. This balanced reception, it should be noted, contrasted with the caricatures published in some newspapers, such as the *Montreal Star* and *Le Canard*. As Chemartin and Pelletier show, the cartoonists ignored the relatively peaceful Canadian and Quebec suffragists, preferring to depict the aggressive masculine suffragettes who came from Britain to corrupt the feminine Canadian soul. In this, they simply reinforced the negative image from which the activists had to defend themselves.

The MSA was officially launched in April 1913. Article 2 of its constitution specified that its main goal was to achieve suffrage, without referring to any particular level of government. In 1915, Derick met with Premier Lomer Gouin, asking him to grant Quebec women the provincial franchise. He firmly refused on the pretext that English women did not possess this right, which seemed to put an end to MSA efforts on winning the provincial franchise. In fact, it is revealing that the group chose to dissolve once the majority of Canadian women were granted the federal franchise in 1918. According to the minutes of its 22 May 1919 general meeting, its dissolution was intended to allow for the creation of another entity, "with a view to bringing about the franchise for women in this province." It kept its distance from the FNSJB, the largest French Canadian feminist association. This was visible in its affiliation with the MLCW, which had no francophone members at the time, its exclusively anglophone executive council, and the fact that it never, so to speak, mentioned the FNSJB and the support it could have provided. For its part, the FNSJB does not seem to have sought a rapprochement either. In other words, it was as if both sides felt that the federal franchise concerned only English Canadian women, perhaps a reflection of worsening ethnic tensions and the increasing sense of alienation among French Canadians.

During its early years, the MSA concentrated largely on organizing conferences, distributing pamphlets, and selling books and booklets on women's suffrage, generally imported from Britain, at annual fairs and exhibitions throughout Montreal and around the province. On 26 November 1913, the *Montreal Herald* published a twenty-page special insert produced by the MSA, in which Montreal, Canadian, and even American feminists, as well as a few men, wrote articles in defence of suffrage. The issue also reported on women's social action and accomplishments, including in the cultural and sports fields, and brought other demands to light. For instance, Lacoste Gérin-Lajoie, the only francophone woman to write an article, denounced the popularity of marriages with separation as to property. She perceived these as less advantageous for women than the matrimonial regime of community property, which she nevertheless wanted to see reformed. Derick, who wrote the editorial, demolished the anti-suffrage arguments one by one. She demanded suffrage for women in the name of their individuality and, above all, their maternal spirit, which was "aroused by infant mortality, the exploitation of child-labor, the evils of prostitution, the hardships of the sweated worker, and the greater value placed upon property than upon the person of women."

Also in the fall of 1913, the MSA came out in favour of extending the municipal vote to married women. At its 2 February 1914 meeting, it showed its determination to make suffrage its sole priority by refusing to back reformist candidates for Montreal elections as a bloc, which the MLCW had asked it to do. Although it agreed to help the MLCW convince female voters to go to the polls, it permitted its members to decide for themselves whether they would support reformist candidates. Around the same time, the MSA executive also adopted a resolution denouncing the force feeding of British suffragettes who were on hunger strike and the practice of freeing them, allowing them to regain their health, and then incarcerating them again.

The outbreak of war in the summer of 1914 slowed the pace of the MSA's initiatives, as it decided to devote its funds to patriotic works. Although it did not abandon all activism, it turned its efforts to current events. Its main preoccupations became the question of women's work in the munitions plants, the rising cost of living, and, at least for the duration of the war, the prohibition of alcohol. In 1917, however, the issue of suffrage re-emerged when the MSA participated in various pan-Canadian mobilization activities to oppose the Wartime Elections Act. The bill for this legislation, which was tabled in the House of Commons on 4 September, granted the vote to women – but *only* if they were military nurses or the close relatives of soldiers serving overseas. Borden had recently invoked conscription, a highly controversial move that triggered a riot in Quebec and was condemned by his political rival, Wilfrid Laurier, leader of the Liberal Party. Now, a federal election lay only a few months away, but conscription had alienated many people, who would certainly not favour Borden at the polls. Determined to stay in power, he solved his problem by the simple expedient of rigging the vote, using the Wartime Elections Act to boost the numbers of Canadians who would cast their ballots for his party. The women whom it enfranchised would naturally support conscription – and the government that had introduced it – because conscription supported their men in the field. Dismayed by the unfairness of the new bill, the MSA executive adopted a resolution stipulating that "the enfranchisement of women should not be based on the qualifications of relatives but on their personal qualifications." It added that "since the proportionate voting for and against conscription would not be altered thereby there was no reason for not giving the vote to all women on the same basis as men." Although they do not go into detail, the minutes of the executive meetings give a good indication that not all MSA members agreed with this position. Some believed that granting the vote to certain categories of women still represented progress and would be an extra guarantee that a Union government led by Borden would be elected, thus protecting conscription, which they also favoured. Despite this dissent, the 14 September MSA general meeting adopted, by a vote of sixteen to eight, a text that restated support for conscription, protested against granting suffrage only to female relatives of enlisted men, and asked that the bill be amended to include all women.

Other pro-suffrage women's associations also experienced internal friction regarding the Wartime Elections Act. As Tarah Brookfield notes in "Divided by the Ballot Box," the bill produced discord across the country, but the conflict seems to have reached a climax in Quebec. In Montreal, French Canadian opposition to conscription degenerated into violent demonstrations, and an April 1918 demonstration in Quebec City left four dead. Although the MSA managed to reach consensus regarding the act, the MLCW ended up supporting it despite the objections of its president, Dr. Grace Ritchie-England. A long-time feminist whose ideas tilted more toward egalitarianism than to maternalism, Ritchie-England decried the Wartime Elections Act. She felt that it discriminated against those who, like her, did not have a son or husband who had gone to war. Furthermore, she thought it was profoundly unjust because it defined women solely in terms of their relationship with men and because the basis on which it enfranchised them differed from that for men.

Ritchie-England did not succeed in convincing the MLCW executive to publicly denounce the Wartime Elections Act. Throughout

OCTAVIA GRACE RITCHIE-ENGLAND
(1868–1948)

The first woman to earn a degree in medicine from Bishop's University (1892) and the third Quebec woman to become a physician, Grace Ritchie practised gynecology, even after her 1897 marriage to Dr. Frank R. England, a surgeon. In 1896, she joined the MLCW, taking charge of its maternal and infant hygiene dossiers. She was also active in the International Council of Women, representing Canada during its 1914 congress in Rome. President of the MLCW when the Borden government unveiled the Wartime Elections Act, she adopted a controversial stance that was strongly opposed by certain member associations. When her term as president (1911–17) ended, she continued the fight for suffrage in the CPSF/PFC. She ran as a Liberal candidate in the Mount Royal riding during the 1930 federal election.

the fall and until the December election that gave Borden a strong majority, she nevertheless continued to criticize conscription and the Wartime Elections Act alongside the Laurier Liberals. In the charged political climate that exacerbated ethnic tensions and polarized the debate, certain MLCW members soon perceived her attitude as anti-patriotic. In the winter of 1918, they tried unsuccessfully to unseat her as president. In the end, Ritchie-England completed her mandate as planned, but this episode shows how deeply the Wartime Elections Act divided the women's movement.

As president of the FNSJB, Marie Lacoste Gérin-Lajoie also felt obliged to speak out regarding the statute. Although her organization had not taken an official position concerning the women's vote in 1917, she stood with Ritchie-England in opposing a measure that she saw as deeply unjust. In a telegram to Borden, quoted by Anne-Marie Sicotte, she asked him to "confer the right to vote on women under the same conditions as men ... in order to recognize the immense services that they have rendered during the war by tending to the wounded, notably in the Red Cross, and performing humanitarian works that honour this country." Unlike Ritchie-England, who invoked sexual equality as a reason for changing the law, Lacoste Gérin-Lajoie sought recognition of the female contribution to the homeland. All women had suffered some sort of sacrifice, not just the wives, daughters, or mothers of men in the military. She returned to the question in her December 1917 *La bonne parole* editorial. As she put it, enfranchising women due to their "derivative value" rather than their "personal value" was simply humiliating. She trenchantly observed that the suffrage offered by the Wartime Elections Act "is less a privilege conceded to [women] than a right granted to soldiers to vote several times through relatives."

Obviously, Lacoste Gérin-Lajoie's suffragism was profoundly at odds with the Borden government's opportunistic exploitation of the women's vote to safeguard conscription, which she, as a nationalist, vigorously condemned. The iniquity of the measure also raised the ire of journalist Éva Circé-Côté. Despite her rather progressive liberal ideas, she had not yet clearly come out in favour of female enfranchisement. Nonetheless, she denounced the statute in the December 1917 issue of *Le Monde ouvrier*, the newspaper of the international unions, to which she contributed regularly under the pseudonym Julien Saint-Michel. She stated, "We are against this government measure, even though we are in favour of the women's vote."

More than granting suffrage only to certain categories of women, the series of pork-barrel schemes instituted by the Borden government to implement conscription seemed to monopolize the attention of French Canadians in the fall of 1917. In the spring of 1918, however, as Ottawa prepared to extend the franchise to the majority of Canadian women, its new statute, titled An Act to confer the Electoral Franchise upon Women, caused an outcry in conservative nationalist circles. In a series of articles published in *Le Devoir* between 28 March and 1 April and subsequently collected in a pamphlet, Henri Bourassa, the paper's founder, attacked the bill with rare virulence. In his second article, which appeared on the front page of *Le Devoir* on 30 March, he wrote, "Parliament, said an old English jurist, can do everything except change a woman into a man, a man into a woman. Yet, it is precisely this impossible task that proponents of women's suffrage have undertaken to perform." In Bourassa's opinion, there was no doubt that "the difference between the sexes brings about the difference in sexual functions," which, logically led to a difference of "social functions." The right to suffrage, which was reserved for men, derived from "the social responsibilities that fall to them ... especially their duties as head of the family." In his often-quoted article of 28 March, he proclaimed, "The main function of woman is and will remain ... maternity, holy and fecund maternity, which truly makes woman the equal of man and, in many respects, his superior." Obviously, therefore, voting was incompatible with the maternal functions of women and was thus a crime against nature. As he explained, "the woman-voter ... will soon engender the woman-conspirator, the woman-floating voter, the woman-procurer of elections, then the woman-member of parliament, the woman-senator, the woman-lawyer – in a word, the woman-man, the hybrid and repugnant monster who will kill the woman-mother and the woman-woman."

In typically outrageous terms, Bourassa was conveying a totally exclusive conception of the roles and functions of men and women and a visceral rejection of any change to this order. As mentioned in the previous chapter, many women shared this vision, including English Canadian women, as shown in the 1912 survey of the *Montreal Star*. In Bourassa's opinion, female enfranchisement could lead only to unhealthy competition between the sexes. Armed with the vote, women would have the same rights as men and would become their rivals rather than their faithful companions. The ultimate result would be the destruction of the family and therefore of society and the French Canadian nation. And there was more: as he expressed it on 30 March, enfranchisement would force all women, even the most respectable ones – the "true" women, as he called mothers – "to wade into the electoral manure ... in order to form a counterweight to the influence of professional suffragettes." Like his grandfather, Louis-Joseph Papineau, Bourassa subscribed to the idea that no normal woman would be caught dead in the political arena.

Also palpable in Bourassa's animosity toward the federal bill, which had just been adopted in the House of Commons, was his bitter sense that yet again, English Canada was about to transform the country's social and political landscape without French Canada's consent. "Our politicians have already ... broken with enough national traditions; shall we, without saying a word, allow them to go so far as to attack the sanctity of our homes, the dignity of our women?" he asked. Unlike many Canadians, including the leaders of the two major federal parties, Bourassa did not believe that women's suffrage would civilize political customs. In his opinion, one need look no farther than the December 1917 election for proof of that. The newly enfranchised women had voted en masse for Borden, who had shamelessly purchased their support by promising that the imposition of conscription would swiftly end the war and bring their men home from the front. They were easily corrupted by the electoral game. As he wrote ironically in his final article, they had "prostituted their electoral franchise, just like vulgar men. And yet, these were the wives of 'heroes'!"

Bourassa accused federal politicians of intrumentalizing the women's vote. But the implacable resistance of French Canadian conservative nationalists to women's suffrage, which strengthened as the 1920s approached, was also based on their desire to use women as a shield for the nation. In a 1919 essay titled "Le féminisme," Monsignor Louis-Adolphe Paquet justified his condemnation of suffrage by stating that "the woman is the joy of the household, the link between families, the strength of traditions, the hope of generations." For the safety of the family, the leavening of the nation, women had to stay away from the polls. This was another way of using them for political purposes.

For Paquet, Bourassa, and many others, suffrage also posed a serious threat because it would feed another pernicious trend: women would push into all the professions that were the exclusive purview of men – a door they had been trying to open for some time. "We are facing an invasion by the female sex, which is fighting the male sex for its most advanced positions," Paquet warned. This was clearly an exaggeration, as the Quebec College of Physicians and the bar still banned women from becoming doctors and lawyers. Not until 1930 and 1941, respectively, were they finally admitted to these professions. Before 1930, the few women who practised medicine in Quebec had to obtain special permission from the Legislative Assembly, a workaround that was not available to those who wanted to practise law. In 1915 and 1916, anglophone and francophone feminists and a few sympathetic male lawyers made representations to the courts and the legislature to force the bar to accept women, but to no immediate effect. Both the courts and the assembly rejected the idea that women might plead cases, for fear that their admission into the legal profession would nourish demands for enfranchisement.

Ultimately, women's suffrage and its inevitable consequences were interpreted not only as a threat to the family and the nation, but as an attack against male identity and supremacy. The gendered division of roles and functions was a necessary bastion in

QUAND MAMAN VOTERA

This 1929 cartoon from *L'Almanach de la langue française* reveals
what happens when Mummy votes – shattered crockery,
domestic warfare, thuggish wives, emasculated husbands,
and traumatized children. In the view of many men, female
enfranchisement would undermine the authority of the head
of the family and hand women power that they might abuse.
This fear was particularly tenacious in Quebec.

their preservation. As historian Susan Mann Trofimenkoff observes in her study of Henri Bourassa, "The debate over the Woman
Suffrage Bill may well have been a debate over the manliness of
the MPs ... Hence the verbal violence of both Bourassa and the
politicians who opposed woman suffrage." One might add that

the fear of losing authority, an eminently masculine attribute, was even stronger among French Canadian nationalists. Already feeling powerless to impose their views on a Canada-wide scale, they were suffering a rather "feminizing" domination. Their opposition to the women's vote can thus be seen not only as an attempt to retain their power in the French Canadian family and nation, but also as a way of pushing back against English Canada by asserting their autonomy of thought and of action – also masculine characteristics. Because female enfranchisement symbolized issues that were largely beyond the control of French Canada, it had a dimension that had never left much room for dialogue. Several of the French Canadian feminists who demanded suffrage were also fervent nationalists, but, like the Irish feminists studied by historian Louise Ryan, they often had difficulty in enlisting support from their comrades. The nationalist claim to self-determination was at least partially grounded in traditional feminine images, which the demand for enfranchisement threatened to topple.

THE COMITÉ PROVINCIAL POUR LE SUFFRAGE FÉMININ/ PROVINCIAL FRANCHISE COMMITTEE

Despite the opposition of conservative nationalists, Quebec women who met the criteria went to the polls in the federal election of December 1921. The imminence of this election, more than the 1918 passage of the female enfranchisement act, seems to have been a catalyst for francophone feminists. Determined to extend the vote to the provincial level, they triggered a debate that quickly reached the height of virulence.

To show how seriously women took their new responsibilities as federal voters, the FNSJB organized a series of civics courses, with the help of the Université de Montréal. As reported in the October 1921 issue of *La bonne parole*, these courses would properly "prepare them to play honourably the role that falls to them in our national destiny." Focusing on both theoretical and practical aspects of electoral democracy, the lecture series appealed to certain clerics who were sympathetic to suffrage. One of these was Father M.-L. Perrin, dean of the philosophy faculty at the Université de Montréal and parish priest of Notre-Dame parish. Perrin maintained that "women's involvement in political elections is an asset to society," that the church "leaves full and entire freedom" of opinion on the subject, and that "no principle, religious or other, is opposed to the suffrage rights of women." Reproduced in the November issue of *La bonne parole*, these words were certainly a balm for the magazine's editors, even though they were immediately denounced by another priest, Father Élie-J. Auclair, director of *La Semaine religieuse de Montréal*. In a 15 November article published in *La Presse*, Auclair claimed that women's suffrage went directly against marital authority, as a woman might vote differently from her husband and thus "cancel out his vote" – something that he found inconceivable.

In the January 1922 issue of *La bonne parole*, Lacoste Gérin-Lajoie assessed the December federal election. She emphasized that 90 percent of the women who were registered on the electoral rolls had turned out to vote, contradicting the idea that francophone Quebec women were not interested in suffrage. She also pointed out that none had encountered violence of any sort at the polling places, an apparently widespread fear, and that the civics courses had attracted almost a thousand participants from many locations and of different social classes. Obviously, women had a strong desire "to give their vote the value of an act of conscience." In Lacoste Gérin-Lajoie's view, the positive experience of the 1921 election and the fact that certain clerics supported suffrage should encourage Quebec women to demand the right to vote provincially. "And now that women know that suffrage is not a religious question," she asked, "will they remain indifferent to obtaining provincial suffrage?"

Her question was rhetorical, as in December 1921 she founded a committee intended to "unify the efforts that will be made to obtain provincial suffrage," as Sicotte reports. This initiative followed a resolution adopted by the FNSJB Central Committee to this end at its 24 November 1921 meeting. In mid-January 1922, a meeting of anglophone and francophone suffragists officially instituted the Comité provincial pour le suffrage féminin/ Provincial Franchise Committee (CPSF/PFC). It was co-chaired by Lacoste Gérin-Lajoie and Anna Lyman, a long-time suffragist who also led the Women's Club of Montreal, an association with a pro-franchise committee. Idola Saint-Jean, who had been active in the fall 1921 campaign to convince women to vote federally, and a certain Mrs. Cushing became the committee's secretaries. Despite the reluctance of some anglophones – including Ritchie-England and Derick, who did not believe that French Canadian women supported suffrage in large enough numbers to convince the government – the CPSF/PFC organized a public meeting for 28 January, which was attended by two hundred people. In early February, a CPSF/PFC delegation went to Quebec City to present the demand to the cabinet. According to Sicotte, even before the meeting, Liberal premier Louis-Alexandre Taschereau had written to Lacoste Gérin-Lajoie to warn her that the clergy was marshalling its opposition. He told her that any bill proposing to extend suffrage to women would no doubt be defeated with "a strong majority." Furthermore, this result would bind the members "when another attempt is made in the future." According to historian Luigi Trifiro, Taschereau's comment about clerical resistance referred to a letter that he had received on 12 January. Signed by all the bishops and archbishops in the province, it expressly asked him to "abstain from granting women the right to political suffrage." However, this warning did not deter the suffragists: on 9 February 1922, between four and five hundred of them – anglophones, francophones, and some representatives of the Jewish community who had founded the

IDOLA SAINT-JEAN
(1880–1945)

Born into a middle-class family, Idola Saint-Jean studied theatre and frequented the city's literary circles. She never married, and she earned her living teaching French at McGill University, where she no doubt met Carrie Matilda Derick. She also taught at the Mechanics' Institute, where members of the anglophone working class gathered. She gave diction courses at the Monument national, which, until 1925, lodged the FNSJB. In 1922, she was among the CPSF/PFC delegates who travelled to Quebec City in the first "pilgrimage" to demand women's suffrage.

More egalitarian than most French Canadian suffragists and more sensitive to the condition of female workers, Saint-Jean created the Canadian Alliance for Women's Vote in Quebec in 1927, which she led until her death. As a columnist for the Montreal Herald, *she strongly denounced the economic, social, and political inferiority of women. She also opined on a number of issues that affected them, particularly in her annual publication,* La Sphère féminine *(1933–45), and on the radio – a new communications tool that Quebec suffragists used widely. The Canadian Alliance participated in the hearings of the Dorion Commission, which examined the legal status of married women in 1929, and the Macmillan Commission, which studied the Canadian banking system in 1934. Between 1933 and 1935, when assembly member Joseph-Achille Francoeur introduced a motion to limit women's access to the job market, Saint-Jean was in the forefront of the fight against it. The first francophone Quebec woman to run for federal office, as an independent Liberal in the riding of Montréal-Dorion-Saint-Denis in 1930, she blazed a trail that Thérèse Casgrain, among others, would follow.*

For the first time in 1922, then fourteen times between 1927 and 1940, a suffrage bill was put before the Legislative Assembly. Suffragists went on "pilgrimage" to Quebec City to hear the debates. Taken in the late 1920s, this photograph shows *(left to right)* Idola Saint-Jean, Antoinette Mercure, and Nora Sampson, of the Canadian Alliance for Women's Vote in Quebec, during their visit to the provincial capital.

National Council of Jewish Women in 1918 – invaded the Legislative Assembly.

Introduced by Liberal member Henry Miles, who sponsored their visit, the delegation's spokespeople, Lacoste Gérin-Lajoie, Lady Drummond, Derick, Saint-Jean, and Thérèse Casgrain – the last two representing a new generation of francophone activists – each took the floor to explain why women should vote provincially. Based on typically maternalist arguments, Lacoste Gérin-Lajoie's plea, reproduced in the February issue of *La bonne parole,* dwelt particularly on their responsibilities in the family and on the difference between the sexes. However, she also recognized the relevance of more egalitarian arguments, giving a good illustration of feminists' overlapping positions:

> It might seem unexpected to you, gentlemen, that I use the woman's family role as an argument to demand her political rights ... as so many apostles of women's suffrage have seen women's ascent to public life only as the consequence of their similarity to men. Without taking anything away from the strength of their arguments, I think, however, that the best argument for women's suffrage is that based on the special and distinctive nature of woman's social function, and it is more in the name of her difference from than her resemblance to men that she must enjoy the electoral franchise.

In suggesting that families were not immune to the effects of "public life" and that women must have a reciprocal influence to better accomplish their maternal duties, Lacoste Gérin-Lajoie was obviously trying to reassure her listeners. Suffrage, she wanted them to understand, would change nothing in the socio-sexual order. Rather, the right to vote, which she deliberately associated with a duty, would simply enable women to "cooperate more effectively in the glorious destiny of our province," but within the strict limits of their sphere of activity.

Lady Drummond's speech was quite similar in tone, but she emphasized the complementarity of men and women in the conduct of both family and social affairs. She added that both sexes made a necessary contribution to the optimal functioning of society. "Our sons will be better men when you have given us the right to vote," she concluded, as reported in *La Presse* on 10 February.

Saint-Jean and Casgrain, on the other hand, seemed more determined to respond to the objections that had long been trotted out by the adversaries of suffrage. Saint-Jean noted that, contrary to what the opponents were peddling, Quebec women obviously wanted to vote, as they had done so in greater proportions than men in the preceding federal election. Nor would it "masculinize" women, as many feared, because they were demanding the franchise in the name of education, public hygiene, and the fight against infant mortality – typically "feminine" issues that came

THÉRÈSE CASGRAIN
(1896–1981)

Thérèse Casgrain was the daughter of Lady Blanche Macdonald and Conservative MP Sir Rodolphe Forget, a lawyer and wealthy Montreal businessman. She married Pierre Casgrain, a lawyer and Liberal MP (1917–41), who was appointed a judge of the Quebec Superior Court. The couple had four children.

During the early 1920s, Casgrain joined the CPSF/PFC and became involved in the struggle for the vote. In 1929, she founded the League for Women's Rights, which pursued this fight alongside Idola Saint-Jean's Canadian Alliance for Women's Vote in Quebec. The same year, she testified before the Dorion Commission to demand a series of changes to the legal status of married women, another area that concerned the League for Women's Rights. Throughout the 1930s, she played a fundamental role in the battle for the provincial franchise, which was finally won in 1940. During the 1940s and 1950s, she ran in nine federal and provincial elections but was never elected. In 1946, she became a candidate for the Co-operative Commonwealth Federation, the ancestor of the New Democratic under provincial jurisdiction. Adopting a more caustic tone, Casgrain refuted the claim that women were not intelligent or educated enough to vote. As she pointed out, many men were hardly geniuses and were generally less educated than their wives, but this did not stop them from casting their ballots. She also ridiculed the notion that elections might cause quarrels between spouses, retorting, "If a man and woman wish to argue, they won't

Party. She was its vice-president and then leader of its Quebec wing, the first Canadian woman to fill such a position.

In 1945, shortly after Ottawa introduced the family allowance cheque, French Canadian nationalists campaigned to have it sent to fathers of Quebec families, not to mothers, as was the case everywhere else in Canada. Casgrain was prominent in opposing their scheme. In the early 1960s, she co-founded the League for Human Rights, of which she was president for several years. She also founded the Quebec branch of the Voice of Women (1961), which promoted peace, and the Fédération des femmes du Québec (1966). In 1970, she was appointed to the senate by Pierre Elliott Trudeau's Liberal government. At the time, she was nine months shy of her seventy-fifth birthday, the mandatory age of retirement for senators. When a journalist suggested that she might not achieve much during her short stay in the Red Chamber, she is said to have replied, "Young man, you'd be surprised what a woman can do in nine months!"

wait until elections take place every five years." In short, unlike their elders, the two youngest delegates were not content simply to plead respectfully for the vote. They took a more rebellious tack, devoting part of their speaking time to trouncing and even deriding the arguments of their adversaries.

However, the suffragists' speeches, like the petition containing more than 3,200 names that they provided to support their demand, were not enough to convince Premier Taschereau. Although he was ready to allow the members and ministers of his party to vote freely when the question was decided in the Legislative Assembly, he himself, he said, was opposed to women's suffrage. He did not see what women could gain from it, and he stressed that it was incompatible with the maternal mission that Lacoste Gérin-Lajoie had described. In addition, it "would deprive [women] of the elevated position in which God Himself had placed them" – words that *Le Devoir* was obviously more than happy to report. He also observed that female enfranchisement was limited to the Anglo-Saxon countries. Significantly, countries in the Latin (and, it was understood, Catholic) tradition, such as France, Italy, Spain, and Belgium, which Quebec most resembled, had not taken this step.

Thus, Taschereau tied suffrage not only to the differences between men and women but to those between Canada's two main ethnic groups – or "races," as they were called at the time. According to the list published in *La Presse*, the vast majority of groups that had gathered signatures for the CPSF/PFC petition were anglophone. At least two French Canadian associations, the young women's section of the Syndicat ouvrier catholique and the Fédération des femmes canadiennes-françaises, both based in Hull, had sent petitions to Taschereau, asking that the vote not be granted to women. For good measure, he tabled in the assembly hundreds of other anti-suffrage petitions, all worded identically, that he had received from every part of the province. Its text, which the francophone newspapers, notably *La Presse*, were eager to publish, appealed to respect for the "Christian spirit of our ancestors," who had never thought of establishing women's suffrage (and for good reason, as parliamentary democracy did not exist in New France). The petition stated that enfranchisement was unnecessary, as it was not justified by any unfolding emergency. And it would inevitably lead to female participation in election campaigns, "a type of activity that is a poor match for the condition of our sex and the duties of the household." Indeed, the petition concluded that the "greatness of woman ... depends neither on the right to vote nor on the right to run for office," and "whatever the political inequalities, they will not be more disadvantageous for us, they will not harm our social influence, any more tomorrow than yesterday and today."

These anti-suffrage interventions were obviously controlled behind the scenes by the ecclesiastical authorities, who wanted to prove that women had no desire to vote. However, the anti-suffrage campaign, which gained momentum as the CPSF/PFC was being consolidated, had been initiated within the Catholic Church itself, as the most conservative clergymen attempted to refute the arguments of their more liberal colleagues, who saw no problem with women voting. For instance, as we have seen, Father Perrin, who had spoken in favour of the franchise in the fall of 1921, was taken to task by Father Élie-J. Auclair. Father Arthur Curotte echoed Auclair's criticism in a series of front-page articles published in *Le Devoir* between 20 and 24 December 1921. In essence, Curotte stated that the demand for female enfranchisement flowed from the idea of universal suffrage, itself inspired by Jean-Jacques Rousseau's social contract theories, which the church had condemned. Thus, he was rejecting the very principle of universal suffrage. His hostility was fiercer, however, when it came to women. Unlike men, they had no "natural" political rights, because they were subjected by divine law to the authority of their husbands. Curotte's ideas were denounced in their turn by Father Ceslas Forest, a Dominican who was also a professor in the philosophy faculty at the Université de Montréal. Publishing his own series of articles in *La Presse* during January and February 1922, he set out to demonstrate that the enfranchisement of women had nothing to do with religion. It was simply a legal matter to be decided by the civil authorities. The bishop of Montreal, Georges Gauthier, adopted a relatively conciliatory attitude. He opposed the women's vote for social reasons but did not make it a point of doctrine. Bishop Joseph-Médard Émard of Valleyfield took a firmer stance. He refused to sign a letter in which the episcopate officially denounced women's suffrage, hoping that this would delegitimize the pro-suffrage movement. Obviously, the clergy did not speak with one voice on the subject of the female franchise.

Nevertheless, the members of the high clergy, including the archbishop of Quebec City, Paul-Eugène Roy, a steadfast opponent of the vote for women, exerted great influence on Catholics in Quebec, and they knew how to use their prestige and authority to shape public opinion. As the CPSF/PFC continued its awareness-raising campaign among the female population and politicians – gaining the support, for example, of Athanase David, provincial secretary – its adversaries multiplied their arguments and encouraged the public to sign anti-suffrage petitions. On 18 February 1922, the newspapers published a letter of congratulations from Archbishop Roy to "the members of the Comité de propagande contre le suffrage féminin," an association that he probably started. Even as he commended the group for its campaign, "which responds perfectly to the views of the entire provincial episcopate," he stated that "legislation opening the door to women's suffrage would be a strike against the fundamental traditions of our race and our faith," thus implying that the question was a point of doctrine. For their part, *Le Devoir* and *L'Action catholique*, both closely affiliated with conservative nationalist and clerical circles, also conducted an ardent anti-suffrage crusade, encouraging women of all classes to organize and circulate petitions. According to Lacoste Gérin-Lajoie, most of these "counter-petitions" were actually launched by priests, who passed them around for signing after giving sermons in which they falsely insinuated that the Catholic Church was opposed to suffrage. Some lay people adopted similar tactics. For instance, the superintendent of public education, Cyrille Delage, asked teachers and students at the École d'enseignement supérieur, the first – and, at the time, the only – classical college for girls, to endorse an anti-suffrage petition. Lacoste Gérin-Lajoie tried to put women on guard against falling "into a trap." Writing for liberal newspapers such as *La Presse,* she advised them to be well informed before signing any petition. But she would experience trouble in fighting the ecclesiastical authorities and the united nationalist leaders. On 9 March, as the legislative session was ending, member Henry Miles presented a bill to enfranchise Quebec women. In response, Premier Taschereau managed to table a petition signed by twenty-three thousand women, a record number for Canada, that opposed the measure. The assembly did not vote on the bill. Instead, after Miles gave a speech to promote it, a member proposed a motion of adjournment, which was adopted immediately. The delegation of women who had come to hear the debate and to support Miles went home empty-handed. It was the first time, but it would not be the last.

In a desperate attempt to rally the episcopate to her side, Lacoste Gérin-Lajoie wrote to all the bishops on 25 February 1922. Hoping to reassure them, she re-emphasized the suffragists' attachment to the role of women in the family. But it was a lost cause: the bishops lined up behind Archbishop Paul-Eugène Roy of Quebec City. Lacoste Gérin-Lajoie duly received a letter from the vicar-general of the diocese of Rimouski, who spoke on behalf of Bishop Léonard, as Sicotte reports. It stressed that "women are our last bastion in a society tormented and troubled by the revolutionary spirit." According to Trifiro, the writer added, "We feel the need to stand guard for our mothers to keep this ill wind from blowing turmoil into their minds and hardening their hearts, reservoir of the virtues of the race and the hopes of the religion."

In the bishops' minds, women were the ultimate weapon against the socio-economic disruptions that were cheating French Canadians of their heritage, and this justified the denial of their democratic rights. The values that they transmitted were strongest in rural Quebec, so the clergy as a whole concentrated its anti-suffrage efforts in those regions. It must be said that the church could most easily influence the population there, just as rural women were no doubt more receptive to a glorified image of femininity that idealized their own lives.

In contrast, linking suffrage to the resolution of social problems – an argument more easily associated with the city than the country – was probably not greatly appealing to rural women. And the middle-class origins of the suffragists helped to deepen the chasm between them. If rural women, and notably members of the Cercles de fermières, associations created by the Quebec government in 1915, did not back feminist demands, it was also because clerical propaganda associated feminism with the destruction of the family. It insisted that the family was the pillar of society and repeatedly told women that they were essential to it. By extension, this logic implied that women were actually at the centre of society and that only by remaining at the centre of the family could they retain their prestige and influence. In short, although the clergy's hold over minds could explain the suffragists' lack of success outside of Montreal, it must also be noted that women who supported their parish priest saw themselves more in his discourses than in those of the feminists, who were not really trying to reach out to them.

In Lacoste Gérin-Lajoie's view, women were disinclined to demand the vote solely because the Quebec clergy associated suffrage with an "anti-social and anti-Catholic doctrine." If that obstacle were swept away, they would be free to join the campaign for suffrage. So she decided to appeal to a higher authority – the pope – and to ask him for a pontifical directive that would confirm the Catholic Church's approval of enfranchisement. Pope Benedict xv had died in January 1922 and been succeeded by Pius xi. Some clerics, including Father Perrin, maintained that Pope Benedict xv, who died in January 1922, had favoured women's suffrage. According to Perrin, who was quoted in *La bonne parole*, Benedict had said, "Not only do I wish that women vote, but I would like to see them vote everywhere." Lacoste Gérin-Lajoie found this encouraging and thought that the new pope, Pius xi, would hold the same view.

In May 1922, she set off for Rome to attend the congress of the International Union of Catholic Women's Leagues (iucwl), with which the fnsjb was affiliated. She also hoped to obtain an audience with the pope, or at least a directive concerning the suffrage question. She had written to him from Montreal, asking him to clarify his position, and had stressed the particular situation of Quebec, a majority Catholic province in a Protestant country. She explained that excluding Quebec women from the vote "is extremely serious, as Quebec is the home of Catholicism in Canada. Is not the abstention of Catholic women from public life, at a time when Protestant women sit in Parliament and influence the legislation, a shameful omission?" As Trifiro notes in his article regarding this issue, she did not hesitate to "play the Catholic influence card" – or, more specifically, the Catholic versus Protestant card – in her attempts to persuade him. During her stay in Rome, she had two audiences with the pope. At the same time, she participated in the work of an iucwl commission that dealt with training women for their civic duties. She hoped that it would generate a text that clearly stated the right of Catholic women to participate in political life. Disappointingly, the commission issued two rather vague resolutions that did not address the subject directly. Worse yet, in absolute contravention of the rules for IUCWL deliberations, when it came time to debate the conclusions of their work in a general session, she found that a third, brand-new resolution had been added to the other two. As Trifiro reports, this third resolution stipulated "that all new initiatives, in the field of women's suffrage, be submitted in advance in each country for approval of its episcopate." Lacoste Gérin-Lajoie later learned that it had been appended at the last minute due to a request by Cardinal Merry del Val, the papal delegate to the IUCWL. He had even dictated it. Further, she discovered that Henri Bourassa had been in Rome at the time and had contacted the IUCWL president. She had told him that suffrage was not a priority in her view, except in cases where it might be used to hinder the designs of left-wing parties that were hostile to Catholicism. No such threat was imminent in Quebec, and Bourassa did everything possible to ensure that the suffrage issue would be subject to the wishes of local churches. In fact, adding the third resolution was his idea. He had known Cardinal Merry del Val for a long time and had suggested the resolution to him, even though it had not been debated beforehand. Very likely, Bourassa had been following the instructions of the Quebec episcopate, whose spokesperson he had become.

Perceiving that she had been outmanoeuvred and that she could not obtain the support of all Quebec bishops for suffrage, Lacoste Gérin-Lajoie resigned as co-president of the CPSF/PFC in November 1922, though she remained an active member. In fact, she took this step mainly to keep the FNSJB, of which she was also president, from being associated with the highly controversial demand for suffrage. Thérèse Casgrain became the new CPSF/PFC co-president. The FNSJB continued to promote the civics courses that the Université de Montréal offered again between 1923 and 1927, responding to the wish of the IUCWL that women be better prepared for their civic duties. These courses, some of which were given by Lacoste Gérin-Lajoie, covered the more technical aspects of voting, but in 1924 they also began to address broader social questions. As Yolande Cohen and Chantal Maillé report, the FNSJB advertising for the courses stated that they were intended "to train in Montreal an elite group of women who are well informed and capable of exerting a positive influence on society." According to Cohen and Maillé, many of the chosen themes, which revealed inequalities in status and rights between men and women, probably helped to awaken the feminist consciousness of attendees.

Lacoste Gérin-Lajoie also retained her interest in the municipal franchise. In the early 1920s, as a commission studied proposals to amend the Charter of Montreal, and again in 1926 and 1927, she joined with the Montreal Women's Club, the Ligue des femmes propriétaires, the MLCW, the CPSF/PFC, and the Canadian Alliance for Women's Vote in Quebec, recently founded by Idola Saint-Jean, to demand that married female property owners be granted the right to vote municipally in Montreal. This request, supported by the Montreal Suffrage Association in the 1910s, was put back on the agenda by the Montreal Women's Club in early 1926, when a delegation of its members appeared before the legislative committee of the municipal council to obtain support for the demand. The representations made by the diverse associations and delegations in Quebec City, to both the Legislative Assembly and the Legislative Council, bore no immediate fruit, however. Only at the end of 1931 did property-owning women who had separation as to property win the right to vote in Montreal civic elections. The extension of the franchise, enshrined in a provincial statute, became effective in 1932, when it was endorsed by the Legislative Council. Those who owned property communally with their husbands would have to wait until 1941.

Lacoste Gérin-Lajoie faced increasing opposition from Bishop Gauthier. As mentioned above, he had adopted a somewhat conciliatory stance regarding suffrage, but now he seemed to change his mind. In 1927 and 1928, inexplicably, he made public declarations in which he condemned all women's action aimed at obtaining the vote. "Women's suffrage is not a panacea against the evils of society," he stated in 1927, as reported by Sicotte. The following year, he opined that "woman must leave politics to devote herself to her family" and that "feminism is a disease [that] needs to be cured by works other than politics." Had he hardened his position because he felt threatened by the arrival of new feminists who were more determined and less in thrall to the church, as Sicotte suggests? Several years before, she reveals, he had written to a Roman prelate that "the women's vote, which in other countries may be useful to the Church, would have no use here for the moment." This comment shows very clearly that the church's stance regarding suffrage depended on its own imperatives and was not grounded in the defence of doctrine or the promotion of human rights. As mentioned above, the Catholic Church in France opposed female enfranchisement at the beginning of the twentieth century. After the First World War, however, it changed its view precisely because it believed that women would share its repugnance for republican candidates and would vote for the anti-republicans that it favoured. The most left-wing French political parties, and even some feminists, also opposed suffrage for the same reason, which explains why French women did not obtain the vote until the end of the Second World War. As we shall see in the next chapter, the members of the Legislative Assembly who debated the franchise in the 1930s were similarly influenced by considerations that had nothing to do with the intrinsic merits of the measure.

⌘

Unlike in Canada as a whole or in the other provinces, it was not until the turn of the 1920s that French Canadian suffragists in Quebec mobilized, with their anglophone sisters, to demand the vote. However, French Canadian nationalists immediately united in resisting it, adopting even more intransigent positions than in the past. In fact, the victory of the English Canadian suffragists between 1916 and 1925, like that of British and American women, seems to have encouraged nationalists to double down on their position to highlight the unique nature of the collectivity that they sought to defend. In reality, the question of suffrage challenged both their ethnicity and their virility, two foundations of their identity for which they would fight to the last breath.

It is as impossible for lawmakers in Quebec City to refuse women their just and legitimate rights as to stop Niagara Falls.

– IDOLA SAINT-JEAN, *MONTREAL HERALD*, 27 FEBRUARY 1930

The right to participate in national activities ... is no more incompatible with our sex, our duties, and our responsibilities than are, for example, the obligation to pay our income taxes and to obey the law ... Claiming that a woman who votes is abnormal is a bit out of bounds.

– THÉRÈSE CASGRAIN AT THE CONGRESS OF LIBERAL WOMEN, OTTAWA, 1928

FOUR

WINNING THE
PROVINCIAL FRANCHISE

WOMEN BRAVE COLD SEEKING VOTE

The two ladies, shown above, paraded the streets of Montreal today drawing attention, through sandwich boards, to the fact that women are allowed to vote in Federal elections but not in Provincial. They made a tour of the main streets and marched around the court house and city hall despite the cold day. The signs were in French and English.

Unlike in Great Britain and the United States, the demand for women's suffrage in Quebec, or even in Canada, was typically not accompanied by major public demonstrations. This photograph, of two "sandwich-board" women on a Montreal street in December 1929, is therefore even more remarkable. The sandwich-board campaign was funded by American suffragist Carrie Chapman Catt. Interestingly, the text on the English-language board is clearer and more demanding than that on the French-language board.

AFTER A FIVE-YEAR PAUSE, the fight for women's suffrage picked up again in the late 1920s. This time, the movement was led by militant feminists who were less beholden to the Catholic clergy – which, at any rate, was now taking more of a background role. The creation of the Canadian Alliance for Women's Vote in Quebec (CAWVQ) by Idola Saint-Jean in 1927 and of the League for Women's Rights (LWR) by Thérèse Casgrain two years later revealed the division in the suffragist movement. Nevertheless, these organizations co-ordinated their activities and received support from older groups, such as the suffrage committee of the Montreal Women's Club, led by Isabella Scott. For their part, the adversaries of the women's vote, including members of the Legislative Assembly who voiced their opinion just about every year in the legislature, continued to hammer home the same ideas as their predecessors. Enfranchisement was also regularly brought up in the assembly, by both proponents and opponents, in connection with the legal status of wives, the adoption of social measures for female workers and mothers, and women's access to the job market and professions. More than ever, the political rights of women were closely linked to their economic and social rights, an overlap that was obviously not unrelated to the economic crisis of the Great Depression.

NEW ASSOCIATIONS, NEW STRATEGIES
Weakened by the departure of Marie Lacoste Gérin-Lajoie from its presidency and by the rebuff from the Quebec government, the Comité Provincial pour le Suffrage féminin/Provincial Franchise

Committee (CPSF/PFC) held only two meetings between 1923 and 1925, and it took no actions. It stirred from its torpor in 1926, when the Montreal Women's Club attempted to obtain the municipal franchise for married property-owning women, but it really came back to life early in the following year. The Quebec executive committee of the Trades and Labor Congress of Canada planned to send a delegation to Quebec City for its annual meeting with the provincial government. Among other things, it intended to demand the women's vote. The possibility arose that members of the CPSF/PFC might accompany it.

Historian Jacques Rouillard observes that the labour delegation had never before permitted representatives from other associations to attend this meeting, during which it normally made its own demands known. The gesture testified to the support of the American-based, and therefore secular, unions for the suffragist cause. Although the Catholic unions, following the directives of the ecclesiastical authorities, opposed suffrage, the "international" unions, some of whose leaders subscribed to a social-democratic ideology, were more inclined to accept it. Joseph-Alphonse Rodier, a journalist and activist in the Montreal Trades and Labor Council (MTLC), had been among the first labour leaders to openly support female enfranchisement. Writing in *La Patrie* on 21 June 1906, even before the Montreal Local Council of Women (MLCW) had officially endorsed enfranchisement, Rodier referred to the "slightly noisy agitation" of the British suffragettes as a sign that suffrage was "a reform that is necessary to all democracies and [that] it will have to apply sooner or later." In 1916, an MTLC resolution supported the eligibility of women to run for positions on school boards. The following year, the MTLC included female enfranchisement at the federal and provincial levels among the three major measures that it was demanding for the post-war period, along with a minimum wage and an eight-hour workday. In 1919, it recommended "the recognition of the political and civil rights of women," which

JOSEPH-ALPHONSE RODIER
(1852–1910)

Born in the United States, where his father had taken refuge after the rebellions of 1837–38, Joseph-Alphonse Rodier was a typographer who was an activist in the Knights of Labor and international unions. He was a main founder of the Montreal Trades and Labor Council (1886) and the Labour Party (1899). A columnist at La Presse *(1898–1903) and* La Patrie, *he promoted progressive ideas that can be called social-democratic, such as compulsory education, the creation of a governmental public education department, the establishment of public health care and old-age insurance, the nationalization of public utilities, and universal suffrage for both women and men.*

led it to support the suffragists during their presentations to the provincial government in 1922. Gustave Francq, MTLC president in 1909 and founder of the weekly *Le Monde ouvrier,* launched in 1916, wrote a number of editorials that favoured the women's vote. He also published columns by journalist Éva Circé-Côté (under her pseudonym Julien Saint-Michel), who, as we have seen, vigorously supported the suffragists. In 1927, he printed the transcripts of some radio talks by Idola Saint-Jean, then leader of the CAWVQ.

Although part of the labour movement supported women's suffrage, feminist organizations did not have much contact with sympathetic unions before the late 1920s. The class difference between feminists and members of the labour movement was no doubt a major obstacle, as was the fact that no Quebec labour association was headed by a woman, with whom feminists might have formed an alliance. According to Marie Lavigne and Michèle Stanton-Jean, Idola Saint-Jean attempted to create a rapprochement between labour and the CPSF/PFC, whereas Maryse Darsigny states that the effort originated with the MTLC. Regardless, the CPSF/PFC leaders were not enthusiastic, leading to fairly bitter discussions. Darsigny reports that some wondered how many delegates they should send to the labour meeting. Others, including Cécile Léger, president of the executive council, and Henriette Tassé, secretary, felt that forming a separate delegation would be wiser. Obviously, linking their organization with male unionists was not unanimously accepted, even though some activists, such as Marion Grant de Rouen, shared Saint-Jean's conviction that workers would be their staunchest allies.

In the end, the CPSF/PFC decided to join the labour delegation, which met with the premier in January 1927. Saint-Jean, Antoinette Mercure, the wife of a Montreal alderman, and Nora Sampson, a CPSF/PFC founder, attended the gathering. According to the 19 January edition of *Le Canada,* the union demands dominated the discussion, and the women notified the premier that they would soon ask for another meeting to better plead their cause. This was scheduled for a month later. In the meantime, Saint-Jean had left the CPSF/PFC to found the CAWVQ, taking some CPSF/PFC members with her. Her decision to establish the new group was based on the lack of combativeness of the CPSF/PFC and its inability to reach out to working-class women, some of whom had asked her to assume leadership of the struggle. She may also have been disappointed at not having been elected francophone president of the CPSF/PFC executive in January 1927. That position went to Cécile Léger, who won on a third ballot. Thus, two suffragist delegations met with the premier on 19 February 1927. According to the 21 February issue of *Le Devoir,* several of the CAWVQ delegates who spoke were members of the Jewish, Polish, Italian, or Irish communities of Montreal. The paper also noted the presence of Louis Morin, a representative of the international unions, and reported on the squabble over precedence that broke out among representatives from the two feminist associations. Saint-Jean did not appreciate having to speak after the CPSF/PFC president. After all, as she pointed out, the meeting had been set up because she took the initiative.

Although it divided the movement and brought out certain ideological and strategic disagreements among the suffragist leaders, the foundation of the CAWVQ also shook up the CPSF/PFC, which became the League for Women's Rights (LWR) in 1929. As its name indicates, the new group had broadened its objectives and would no longer confine itself solely to campaigning for enfranchisement. According to its constitution, its various targeted reforms would produce "an equal opportunity in the social, political, civil, and economic fields" for both sexes. Founded and led until 1942 by Thérèse Casgrain, the LWR proclaimed itself a fully secular organization and advocated a more egalitarian and individualistic feminism than did the FNSJB. Nevertheless, it continued to emphasize the differences between the sexes and the maternal function of women. As we shall see, the CAWVQ, through Saint-Jean's voice, also believed that equality and difference could coexist, but it put less emphasis on the subject of maternity. More than the LWR, it sought to align itself with working-class women, whose struggles it supported. At its 29 April 1940 congress, which coincided with the suffrage victory, five thousand female garment workers gave Saint-Jean an ovation to thank her for her commitment, according to *La Presse*. Until then, the feminist movement had seen these women mainly as potential beneficiaries of its charity, rather than allies in the struggle. It is difficult to know what roles female workers may have played in the CAWVQ, however, as the activists we know about came mainly from the middle class.

For its part, the LWR rejected the idea that it represented or worked only for the better-off. "We do not work for our own gain," its 1932–33 annual report stated, "but to emancipate from an

Produced by the League for Women's Rights, this poster
demonstrates that the demand for the franchise was grounded
in maternalist logic. In helping to choose elected representatives,
as these babies are demanding, women could force the assembly
to adopt laws favourable to the welfare of children, whose needs
they knew best.

unjust and painful situation women less fortunate than us and
less well situated to defend themselves." In fact, it participated in
many of the great struggles that aimed to improve the lot of female workers and disadvantaged women. For instance, with the
CAWVQ, and like the FNSJB before it, it demanded – unsuccessfully
– that at least one woman sit on the Women's Minimum Wage
Commission. Created in 1925, six years after the law instituting it
had been passed, the commission was charged with setting wage
scales in certain sectors of female employment. Several provinces
had already founded their own commissions, in an attempt to
counter the overexploitation of women workers. Feminist associations obviously felt that the commission should have a female
member so that women's interests would be better represented.

Despite the pressure exerted by the FNSJB, and then by the LWR and the CAWVQ, the government steadfastly refused to appoint a woman, no doubt because doing so would have given those groups too much power. In 1927, Casgrain nevertheless played an important role in the commission as a representative of the public, a position that Saint-Jean would occupy in the early 1930s.

In 1933, the LWR began to push for the Quebec Women's Minimum Wage Act to apply to teachers, as the hardships of the Depression had caused numerous rural school boards to cut their salaries or even stop paying them. The government acceded to this demand in 1935. Conditions did not improve much, however, as the school board commissioners – all of them men – often paid only the minimum recommended salary, without regard for teachers' experience. The LWR also supported the principle of equal pay for equal work, but like the FNSJB, it felt that women's paid employment had to be defended as an economic necessity, not as an absolute right. In contrast, the CAWVQ felt that access to the job market was a right – that "of living and enjoying dignity and independence." Furthermore, just as men could not be forced to work in a single trade or profession, the role of homemaker could not be prescribed for all women: "What would one think of a law that forced all men to practise the same profession or trade? Do we not commit the same absurdity by trying to condemn all women to marriage, permitting them no function other than maternity?"

Saint-Jean published this statement in the 1935 issue of *La Sphère féminine,* the CAWVQ magazine. At the same time, she was organizing a campaign to quash a motion tabled in the Legislative Assembly by Liberal member Joseph-Achille Francoeur. Its intent was to diminish the numbers of women in the workforce. If it passed, only those women whose income was essential to their or their family's survival could legally be paid a salary. In his view, this was the only way to counter male unemployment, which was reaching peak numbers at the time. In 1933, when Francoeur first tabled his motion, about a third of the male workforce in Montreal was jobless. This situation resulted in widespread urban poverty and some social unrest. It also upset the socio-sexual order, all of which unnerved the political class. It was only in 1935, however, that Francoeur's bill was called to a vote. As a protest, the CAWVQ convened a vast assembly at which various well-known men and women, both francophone and anglophone, including some representatives of the LWR, denounced the measure. According to the 1 February issue of *Le Canada,* numerous speakers emphasized that women rarely worked for their pleasure or to pay for luxury items, as Francoeur and his supporters claimed. Many defended women's individual freedom to have a job. Others linked the lack of female enfranchisement in Quebec with the tabling of such a motion, which, in their view, could never have been presented otherwise.

As occurred repeatedly during the 1930s when women's civil or economic rights were discussed, the vote was also brought up. Feminists and their allies had no doubt that enfranchisement would guarantee greater respect for the fundamental rights of women, especially their economic rights. In a sense proving them right, Francoeur himself stated that he had been "elected in Dorion by the men's vote," as *Le Soleil* reported on 14 March 1934, an indication that he felt bound to defend their interests first and foremost. According to *La Patrie,* he also suggested "that it is only since women's labour has been so widespread that there is talk of the women's right to vote, feminist ploys, and the ruin of households." This comment suggests that the crisis of the Great Depression was probably an aggravating factor in the determination of assembly members to bar Quebec women from voting provincially. Or, at least, it may have served as a convenient excuse. Some of their declarations, reported in the reconstructed debates of the Legislative Assembly, confirm this. During the 1933 debate on women's suffrage, Liberal member Augustin-Armand Legault asserted, "It is not in the middle of a crisis that one makes changes as radical as that of giving women the right to vote."

In any case, Francoeur's bill was not adopted. The majority of members felt that it bordered on the dictatorial as it contravened women's freedom to work, even though the jobs they held were generally disdained by men. However, many people continued to insist that the vote was an essential tool to protect the interests of female workers and to achieve various reforms. For instance, in a July 1935 article published in *La Revue Moderne,* Édith Plamondon, a contributor to the magazine, connected the low salaries of teachers to the fact that they were denied the vote and thus "could not make themselves heard." "It is our fault," she added, "because we have not yet been able to make those in government recognize the principle that women need the rights to vote and to run for office to bring about the social reforms that interest them directly."

For feminists in the 1930s, the essential challenge was to convince lawmakers that women should be enfranchised even though large numbers of them were at best indifferent, and at worst hostile, to the measure. The fact that so many women were unsympathetic was little short of a gift for anti-suffrage members, who could simply claim to be honouring the wishes of the majority. If most women did not desire the vote, why should it be forced on them? For instance, the Liberal member for Beauce, Joseph-Édouard Fortin, declared in 1933, "If I vote against women's suffrage, it is because the women in the Beauce are not in favour of the women's vote and the vast majority asked me to come out against the bill. The women in the countryside, whom the champions of suffrage do not consult enough, are against the right to vote." This opinion, which shone a harsh light on the suffragists' main weakness, was shared by various dailies that were happy to drive the point home. *La Presse* certainly did on 21 March 1935, when it noted, "It must be observed that in the province of Quebec the movement remains a campaign launched by a small number of people who have not yet been able to raise backing from the masses."

Newspaper reports tended to show that a good many women were not particularly concerned about being excluded from political citizenship. As a 23 February 1933 editorial in *La Patrie* expressed it,

> The women who are perfectly comfortable with not exercising suffrage do not consider themselves to be in a state of inferiority. To the contrary, most of them contemplate with haughty serenity the machinations of their male contemporaries in the field of politics and find them in no way glorified by the sovereign power that the title of elector theoretically confers.

In other words, the women who opposed suffrage simply did not believe in the democracy in which the suffragists wanted to participate, as they saw the political game as being based on dishonesty and corruption. "Married women in the province of Quebec are not, in general, in favour of the right to vote," declared a Mrs. E. Coff in the April 1933 *La Revue Moderne*, "and with the exception of a very ardent feminist group, this privilege is not the ambition of a great number of us." In fact, some women were apparently troubled by the prospect of participating in politics. In a letter printed in the 9 September 1933 issue of *L'Écho du Saint-Maurice*, a Shawinigan reader stated that women who wanted the vote were those "for whom the home has no attraction, who do not like family life." She concluded, "Let us therefore seek, ladies, to preserve our feminine elegance; let us not seek to become men." Obviously, for this writer, as no doubt for many other women, casting a ballot every four or five years was tantamount to abdicating her femininity, renouncing her image of herself and of "true women," and exposing herself to the inquisitive eyes of men.

This view was also reflected in *Le Devoir*. On 23 February 1933, its parliamentary correspondent, Alexis Gagnon, mocked the assemblymen who supported women's suffrage by calling them "feminizing members." In his view, the suffragists who had come to listen from the galleries were more masculine by comparison, fearsome battle-axes who resembled men. By all evidence, just as in the nineteenth century, the suffrage issue appeared to threaten the gender identity of both sexes. Was it merely a coincidence that this type of remark seemed particularly common in 1933, the worst year of the Depression? Large numbers of men were now condemned to unemployment and could no longer play the traditional male role of breadwinner, a loss that jeopardized their sense of masculinity. It is difficult to say with certainty, but such comments give a good indication that resistance to the women's vote was still very much alive and that it remained based on the same fears. Convincing women that casting a ballot would not harm their femininity thus became a main task for feminists.

Unlike the CPSF/PFC, which had never really made it a priority, the LWR and the CAWVQ now reached out to women all over the province, especially through radio broadcasts, to persuade them of the need for suffrage and its potential benefits. In 1931, the LWR inaugurated a weekly fifteen-minute program on radio station CKAC, on which the guests discussed suffrage as well as other issues involving the political, social, and legal condition and status of women in Quebec and elsewhere. The previous year, the CAWVQ had obtained air time on radio station CFCF for a show called *Les Droits des femmes/The Rights of Women,* and in 1933 it launched another weekly program called *L'Actualité féminine,* transmitted in English and French on alternating weeks. This was broadcast on CHLP, then CKAC. Idola Saint-Jean spoke on the program to denounce not only the provincial and municipal disenfranchisement of women, but also their inferior legal and economic status. In 1937, Thérèse Casgrain began to host a Radio-Canada program named *Fémina,* also in French and English. It featured discussions on various topics and sketches illustrating social, civil, and professional discrimination against Quebec women. According to the LWR annual report for 1937–38, "These programs were very effective in providing information to the population."

In theory, the radio programs, which remained on the air until women obtained the vote, reached a large female audience that was dispersed over a vast territory and provided popular education at a low cost. The LWR received numerous letters from all over the province asking for more information or transcripts of the talks given on air – testimony to the impact of and interest in these programs. Nevertheless, few households owned a radio during the 1930s, especially in regions where electricity was not always accessible. Thus, neither the CAWVQ nor the LWR could be content with this means of informing women and convincing them to demand the vote. Their leaders, including Florence Fernet-Martel, who also hosted *Fémina*, Ethel A. Bielby from the LWR, and Saint-Jean from the CAWVQ, frequently visited remote areas of the province to distribute pamphlets and run information booths at agricultural fairs.

In the summer of 1927, *Le Bulletin des agriculteurs* published reports by Irène Joly, who was also travelling the province to give talks on the women's vote and to establish local sections of the Fédération provinciale pour le suffrage féminin, a group that she led. Her tour seems to have roused opposition from the clergy and other members of the male elite in certain towns, as indicated in the 28 July issue of *L'Action populaire*. In the reports that she sent to the *Bulletin des agriculteurs*, however, Joly emphasized her generally sympathetic reception and the fact that everywhere she went, she succeeded in starting a local committee of her federation. No doubt to avoid accusations of partisanship, she tried to place these committees under the co-leadership of two women who belonged to or supported the two major national political parties. On one occasion, she even managed to recruit the secretary of the local Cercle des fermières, which shows that not all members of these groups were hostile to suffrage despite the claims of their directors. It is difficult to uncover which actions these newly founded committees took and with what results, though Joly's federation did participate in several of the annual "pilgrimages" to Quebec City. Her commitment reminds us that though the LWR and the CAWVQ played a key role in the fight for suffrage, they were not the only groups to support it. They were joined by the Association des femmes conservatrices de la ville de Québec, founded by Thaïs Lacoste-Frémont (Marie Lacoste Gérin-

FLORENCE FERNET-MARTEL
(1892–1986)

Florence Fernet was one of the earliest graduates of the École d'enseignement supérieur, which was founded by the nuns of the Congrégation Notre-Dame as Quebec's first classical college for women. After earning a literature degree from Université Laval de Montréal in 1912, she became an English teacher and then a secretary and translator. In the 1930s, after her marriage and the birth of her son, she became interested in the suffragist cause and was elected French-language secretary of the League for Women's Rights in 1937. A contributor to the radio program Fémina, she also travelled the province to distribute pro-suffrage literature, and she helped with the struggles to reform the Civil Code, to admit women to the bar, and to have family allowance cheques, established by Ottawa in 1945, sent to mothers. During and after the war, she held various positions in the federal and provincial civil service. She was also a founder of the Montreal section of the Canadian Federation of University Women (1949), an active member of the Fédération des femmes libérales du Québec, and a writer for magazines such as Châtelaine.

Lajoie's sister), groups of Liberal women who were affiliated with the Liberal Party of Canada, the Montreal Women's Club, the Montreal Local Council of Women, and the international unions. Like Joly's federation, the LWR attempted to create local sections but was not very successful. The CAWVQ seems to have limited most of its activities to the greater Montreal region, as the female workers whom it wanted to represent were concentrated

IRÈNE JOLY
(1875–1967)

Although she is not a well-known figure in the history of Quebec feminism, Irène Joly was nevertheless a vigorous activist. Born in Montreal to French parents, she established a private business school, the Institut sténographique de France, in 1912, where she taught stenography and typing. She gave similar courses at the Monument national, where she no doubt became acquainted with the leaders of the FNSJB. She founded the Quebec section of the Fédération des femmes conservatrices and the Ligue des femmes propriétaires de Montréal. Established in 1925, the latter fought to obtain the municipal franchise for married property-owning women. A member of the women's section of the Ligue pour le progrès civique à Montréal, Joly also gave radio talks and published a number of articles in dailies and women's magazines, notably on female enfranchisement at the municipal and provincial levels. When, at the request of various feminist groups, the Dorion Commission was set up in 1929 to examine the legal status of married women, she appeared at its hearings on behalf of the Ligue des femmes propriétaires.

there. Both associations nevertheless hammered home their message on the air, in the newspapers, in women's and feminist magazines – including *La Sphère féminine,* founded by the CAWVQ in 1933 – in pamphlets and posters that they produced and distributed, and in public speeches. All of this helped to convince a constantly growing share of the population that suffrage was needed. In 1938, during a trade fair in the Sun Life Building in Montreal, the LWR handed out more than twenty thousand pamphlets that explained why it was demanding suffrage. It also organized a poll, directed by Mayor Adhémar Raynault, to learn how visitors to the trade fair felt about women voting. More than eight thousand people were in favour, and fewer than three hundred were against. The same year, the LWR estimated that 70 to 80 percent of rural women were pro-suffrage, as opposed to about 50 percent of rural men. This claim, based on the distribution of pamphlets in a few towns (Sherbrooke, Trois-Rivières, Louiseville, and others), was certainly more impressionistic than scientific and was perhaps overly optimistic. Nevertheless, after a decade of increasingly intensive crusading, public opinion appeared to be turning toward acceptance of enfranchisement, presented as the only way to end the subordinate status of Quebec women.

The propaganda produced by the LWR and the CAWVQ shows that throughout the 1930s, both associations sought constantly to connect the denial of the franchise with the economic and legal inferiority, discrimination, and lower living conditions experienced by Quebec women. Whereas the FNSJB had justified enfranchisement mainly by emphasizing the family, social, and even moral responsibilities of women, the LWR and the CAWVQ presented the vote as a tool that would end the injustices suffered by women as human beings. Thus, the argument of duties was overtaken by the argument of rights, notably access to fundamental economic and social rights. The LWR did show some ambivalence by also associating suffrage with women's responsibilities in the family and society, but during the 1930s, the issue of the vote was more regularly connected to the acquisition of other rights that women still lacked.

Was this type of propaganda enough to convince the most reluctant? A study conducted by historian Aline Charles may supply an answer. In his election campaign of fall 1935, Louis-Alexandre Taschereau promised that Quebec would participate in the federal-provincial pension scheme. During the winter of 1935–36, several hundred women wrote to Taschereau, asking that the pension be paid to their husbands or themselves. In analyzing their letters, Charles found that many cited Christian charity to explain why they should receive the pension. But also, and often at the same time, they referred to it "as a right claimed" because of the taxes they had paid, the children they had raised, or, in the case of single women, the work they had done for the nation. Clearly, not having the provincial franchise did not deter these women from seeing themselves as citizens. They may not have possessed the vote – which they were not asking for – but they seemed to see themselves as part of the body politic and therefore as endowed with certain rights. Perhaps, unlike the feminists, they did not see enfranchisement as the necessary first step in the acquisition of social rights. Or perhaps the feminist struggles and the publicity surrounding them had helped to forge a more demanding spirit among some women, especially as the economic crisis of the Depression made them aware of the state's responsibility toward the most disadvantaged. In other words, the debates around the vote may have encouraged these women to write to their premier. It must also be said that writing such requests was a common tactic throughout Canada. Even before parliamentary democracy had been established or was still in its infancy, various groups, including women and Indigenous peoples, wrote to men in power, asking that their rights be respected or that they be granted privileges.

While seeking the support of the female population, especially rural women, the feminist organizations were also addressing the government authorities, as they alone could enact the laws that they were demanding. One initiative in this regard was to send a ten-thousand-signature petition to King George V on the occasion of his silver jubilee in 1935. This action stressed that in failing to enfranchise women, Quebec was lagging behind the other Canadian provinces and some countries in the British Commonwealth. It was more symbolic than anything, and it had no follow-up, but it was a publicity coup nonetheless. Three years later, representatives of women's groups appeared before the Rowell-Sirois Commission, created by Ottawa to examine economic relations between the federal government and the provinces. On behalf of the CAWVQ, Saint-Jean made a speech in which she expressed her anger that Quebec women paid income tax but could not elect their representatives – an injustice that was clearly unacceptable. In the speech, published in *La Sphère féminine* in 1938–39, she even asked the federal government to legislate the vote for Quebec women. As she explained, "the political and civil status of women in Quebec is against the national interest and it is a question that the federal authorities should occupy themselves with, for it is in conflict with our democratic ideal." For its part, the LWR submitted a brief written by Elizabeth Monk. The brief highlighted the deplorable situation of Quebec women, notably their starvation wages and the high infant mortality rate, which it linked to the absence of suffrage. It also noted that because Quebec women were still excluded from the bar (like Monk herself), they could not sit on federal commissions or occupy legal positions, because those who did generally needed to be lawyers. As a consequence, the LWR asked that the British North America Act be amended to ban the adoption of laws, federal or provincial, that would have the effect, as quoted by Micheline Dumont and Louise Toupin, "of keeping women from exercising civil rights or administrative functions, being appointed to an administrative or judicial position, or fulfilling the duties of or practising all civil trades or professions."

ELIZABETH MONK
(1898–1980)

After taking her law degree at McGill University in the 1920s, Elizabeth Monk passed the Nova Scotia bar exam in 1934, as the Quebec bar still refused women this privilege. In the 1930s, while working for a Montreal law firm, she became the legal counsellor for the League for Women's Rights. She wrote a brief for the Rowell-Sirois Commission, which the commissioners rated as one of the best articulated and reasoned that they received, and it contributed greatly to advancing the cause of suffrage. With Jessie Kathleen Fisher and Lucie Lamoureux-Bruneau, Monk was among the first three Montreal women to sit on municipal council, in 1940. She was also one of the first two women, with Suzanne Raymond Filion, to register with the bar of Quebec when it finally admitted women in 1941.

These appeals to the British Crown and the federal government show that, unlike the FNSJB, for which social and national action by women went hand in hand, the LWR and the CAWVQ were distancing themselves from the traditionalist nationalism of the period. Their religious neutrality, their indifference to the opinions of conservative clerics with regard to women's suffrage, and their numerous critiques of Quebec society – notably, their denunciation of the subordination of women in marriage, the discrimination that they suffered, and the absence of social laws – show that they were far from exalting the French Canadian customs and lifestyles that were so dear to the traditional nationalists who dominated the political landscape. To the contrary, they tended to see tradition as an obstacle to progress, which, in their view, had favoured the emancipation of women everywhere else. This is why they chose to bypass the provincial government and appeal directly to Ottawa, hoping to have some effect. They were not disappointed: according to Catherine Cleverdon, the LWR brief to the Rowell-Sirois Commission not only helped to publicize the deplorable situation of Quebec women but also encouraged the federal Liberal Party to exert pressure on its Quebec wing. This explained the presence of some forty female delegates, including Thérèse Casgrain, at the first orientation meeting ever held by the Liberal Party of Quebec, in June 1938. It was during this meeting that the Liberals promised to enfranchise women once they returned to power, which they did in 1939.

AT THE HEART OF THE STRUGGLE

During the early 1930s, the LWR and the CAWVQ had amplified their attempts to broaden their support, but progress was slow in francophone circles. And ultimately, the politicians in Quebec City held the whip hand, as they alone could amend the electoral statute. The intervention by Casgrain and the other female delegates at the Liberal Party meeting, including active LWR members Renée Vautelet and Florence Fernet-Martel, proved crucial to obtaining the vote, though, ultimately, politicians' support remained the only way to change the law. Every year, either the LWR or the CAWVQ had asked a lawmaker to sponsor a bill that would enfranchise women and enable them to run for office. When the bills were tabled in the Legislative Assembly, a delegation of feminists "invaded" the gallery, as the newspapers put it, to watch the ensuing debate. Even though they left disappointed, and sometimes angry at the misogynous or injurious speeches from members, their "pilgrimages" to Quebec City, as the press dubbed them, gave them high visibility.

The suffragists went to the Legislative Assembly fourteen times between 1927 and 1940, when they finally won their fight (see Table 1). It should be noted that most of the time, the members opined not on the principle of suffrage but on the opportunity to study, in second reading, the content of the bill. In an almost unvarying scenario, the majority voted to delay the second reading by six months, until after the legislative session had ended. Thus, most of the suffrage bills died on the order paper and the suffragists would be forced to start from scratch the next year. In 1936, suffrage was tabled twice: once in the spring, when the Taschereau government, worn out by fifteen years in power, lingered in its final hours, and a second time in the fall, when the newly elected Unionist government of Maurice Duplessis called a special session to revise the electoral law. Realizing that the women's vote was not included among the government's planned modifications, a small delegation led by Casgrain appeared before the parliamentary commission charged with studying the proposed amendments. She suggested that the words "male sex" be removed from article 12 of the electoral statute, a simple change that would enable women to vote. Unionist member Camille Pouliot supported her proposal, but the assembly rejected it. In 1937, on the other hand, no suffrage bill was presented, as the LWR decided to concentrate on its subscription campaign, which would raise the necessary funds to continue the fight.

During the years when the suffragists and their supporters in the Legislative Assembly were working for the women's vote, they made a series of arguments, generally combining equality of rights and difference between the sexes. Thus, their philosophy did not completely differ from that of the FNSJB. But, as mentioned above, whereas the FNSJB had demanded the vote so that women could better accomplish their maternal duties, the feminists of the 1930s felt that equality of rights was also essential for women to be full individuals, however they chose to live. Of course, the maternalist argument was part of the FNSJB strategy. This was implied by FNSJB secretary Georgette Le Moyne, as quoted in the January 1928 *La bonne parole*. She said that she hesitated to evoke women's rights "in order to not alarm certain grief-stricken souls,

TABLE 1: Female enfranchisement bills in the Legislative Assembly, 1927–40

Year	Sponsoring member	Party	Riding	Vote: for/against	(% votes against)
1927	Victor Marchand	Liberal	Jacques-Cartier	13/51	(80)
1928	William Tremblay	Ouvrier-Conservateur	Maisonneuve	11/39	(78)
1929	William Tremblay	Ouvrier-Conservateur	Maisonneuve	16/50	(75)
1930	Irénée Vautrin	Liberal	Saint-Jacques	24/44	(65)
1931	Irénée Vautrin	Liberal	Saint-Jacques	21/47	(69)
1932	Anatole Plante	Liberal	Mercier	33/52	(70)
1933	Anatole Plante	Liberal	Mercier	20/53	(72)
1934	Gaspard Fauteux	Liberal	Sainte-Marie	25/52	(68)
1935	Edgar Rochette	Liberal	Charlevoix-Saguenay	19/43	(69)
1936	Frederick Monk	ALN-Conservateur	Jacques-Cartier	24/43	(61)
1936	Camille Pouliot	Union nationale	Gaspé-Sud	21/49	(70)
1938	Grégoire Bélanger	Union nationale	Montréal-Dorion	16/48	(74)
1939	Pierre-Auguste Lafleur	Union nationale	Verdun	No vote	
1940	Adélard Godbout	Liberal	L'Islet	67/9	(11)

who are saddened when they hear talk of justice, rights, demands for women." The FNSJB discourse nevertheless clearly suggested that its demand for suffrage was built on women's maternal responsibilities, much more than on what they shared with men in terms of humanity. This perspective was accentuated in the 1930s, when the new leaders of the FNSJB seemed to lose interest in suffrage to fall into line with their bishop's directives. For instance, in the May 1940 *La bonne parole,* just after Quebec women had obtained the vote, Yvonne Letellier de Saint-Just rejoiced "at the new testimony of trust that has been placed in women." She concluded, "Participation in the choice of leaders of the nation will enable women to broaden and solidify the rampart that protects the family." Obviously, in her opinion, suffrage was a tool that protected the family, not an individual right symbolic of a truly democratic society.

Although Casgrain and Saint-Jean linked the vote to the maternal role of women to differing degrees, they referred to other feminine models, which they placed on an equal footing. In a speech reproduced in the June 1928 issue of *Mon Magazine,* Casgrain stated, "The trusted counsellor to a husband, the educator of a family, and the free woman who earns her living, pays her taxes, and administers her assets have the incontestable right to say yes or no, at the same time as their fellow citizens of the other sex." In a February 1927 radio talk reproduced in *Le Monde ouvrier,* Saint-Jean asked, "Shouldn't women who are citizens of the province, who contribute to its wellbeing and prosperity as mothers and as teachers, by their intellectual and manual labour, by paying taxes and obeying laws, have all their privileges and rights as citizens?" Whereas FNSJB demands for suffrage did not refer to single working women or women on their own, the LWR and the CAWVQ did not hesitate to evoke their existence alongside the mother of the family. The image of the woman who paid taxes and who therefore merited the right to vote also referred to the idea that parliamentary democracy rested on the liberal principle of "no taxation without representation," which, in all justice, the government should respect.

The principles of justice and equity also encouraged the LWR and the CAWVQ to continue the fight to have women admitted to the bar. This battle began in 1915–16 in an effort to allow Annie Macdonald Langstaff, McGill University's first female law graduate, to practise her profession. A second skirmish blew up during the early 1920s and a third in the early 1930s, under pressure from the LWR. Lacoste Gérin-Lajoie had participated in the 1915–16 engagement but did not get involved this time, but the FNSJB magazine, *La bonne parole,* opened its pages to Casgrain. In an October 1929 article, she traced the history of the struggle and noted, "It is true that this measure would benefit only a minority, but it would establish the fundamental principle of freedom of the professions." In other words, Casgrain justified this demand as a fundamental right of women, as individuals, to pursue the career of their choice. She took the same position with regard to the Francoeur motion. In the same article, however, she stated,

We are perfectly aware that the ideal is the woman at home in her house ... [but] this is unfortunately not the case. The woman has had to leave her home and make her way to the factory, the office, the shop. And so, why refuse her access to higher careers if she has the talent and the capacities to pursue them?

This seems to imply a hierarchy of female roles, with the homemaker positioned at the top but sadly in decline. Many of Casgrain's speeches emphasize that economic transformations had taken women outside the home, an inexorable process to which society had to adjust by granting them, notably, the right to vote. The same type of argument would be voiced by William Tremblay, who sponsored the suffrage bill of February 1929.

Athanase David, the provincial secretary, raised the stakes in 1930 by stressing that allowing women to participate in the public sphere could not be reconciled with denying them the vote by claiming that they had no place in the polling booth. As he put it, "Women have been permitted to work outside of their homes, they have been encouraged to occupy charitable works, they have, in short, been 'externalized' – one cannot now go and tell them that it is for fear of seeing them leave their homes that one is refusing them the right to vote."

Therefore, equal rights – political rights in particular – were to flow from equality of conditions, as women now occupied the public sphere, just like men. In the suffragists' view, even as modern life was removing women from the private domain of the family, the state was invading it by adopting – or refusing to adopt – certain laws that influenced its well-being. A few pro-suffrage members of the assembly justified the enfranchisement of women by claiming that the division between public and private no longer existed. The member for Mercier, Anatole Plante, who sponsored the 1933 suffrage bill, declared, "It is impossible to maintain today that life in the home is completely distinct from our national life."

Without directly referring to the porosity of spheres, Saint-Jean insisted that women were "particularly interested in social legislation" because "the questions of education, public health, housing, women's work, and women's legal status" affected them more than men, as she emphasized in an 18 February 1930 *Montreal Herald* article. Though she did not suggest that outside influences were contaminating the home, she recognized that the concerns of men and women were different. Similarly, though she did not attribute these differences to biology, as many people did, she still felt that women's intervention in public affairs via suffrage could only be beneficial to society as a whole. "The extension of the vote to women," she wrote, "would result in a reduction in the province's mortality rates, improved conditions for education, and adoption of social legislation that would favour mothers and children and give them advantages that are currently denied to them and yet are enjoyed by women in the other provinces of the Dominion." Despite her egalitarian claims, Saint-Jean thus did not completely escape the deeply rooted idea that the sexes were intrinsically different. In fact, all feminists of the period alluded, at one time or another, to the feminine qualities that would "civilize" electoral mores. They would also force the government to adopt laws that were fairer or more sensitive to the needs of women and of the most vulnerable – qualities that a number of pro-suffrage assembly members also evoked. The fact that most laws affecting women's lives directly were under provincial jurisdiction provided even greater justification for allowing them the vote.

The ideas about women's maternal responsibilities also fed into the other great feminist demand of the period: reform of the Civil Code. As early as 1913, Lacoste Gérin-Lajoie had written to Premier Lomer Gouin, asking for changes that would give more autonomy to married women and enable them to better fulfill their duties in the family. Her request was not granted. In 1929, thanks to the intervention by Casgrain, Premier Taschereau finally agreed to institute a commission of inquiry, which was chaired by Judge Charles-Édouard Dorion, to study the question. Taschereau's government was also inclined to take this step because the Civil Code was increasingly being attacked and mocked by anglophones, who considered it medieval, or even despotic. For instance, in a November 1928 *Montreal Herald* article, Isabella Scott, a leader of the Provincial Suffrage Committee of the Montreal Women's Club and honorary president of the CAWVQ, stated that the Civil Code kept married Quebec women in slavery – a claim that startled quite a few people. A year later, the same newspaper published a special issue in which it vigorously denounced the legal incapacity of wives. Its articles were illustrated with caricatures that portrayed the Civil Code as a senile old man.

Montreal Herald, November 1929

This cartoon was one in a series of twelve published in late November 1929, when the Dorion Commission was holding its hearings on the legal status of married women. By depicting the Civil Code as an old man, the *Montreal Herald* implied that it was behind the times, as well as utterly unjust toward women. The presence of the rooster and the hen link Quebec's civil laws with rural society and therefore with backwardness, according to public opinion of the day.

Most Montreal women's associations presented briefs to the Dorion Commission. In essence, they were asking that married women be granted more economic autonomy, including the right to keep their own salaries, that they must grant their consent before their minor children could marry, and that they could act as guardians of children. Overall, these demands, which meant that women would be better able to exercise their maternal duties, were granted. On the other hand, the commissioners refused to abolish the principle of marital power, as the Ligue des femmes propriétaires and the CAWVQ would have liked. Despite the demands of the Montreal Local Council of Women and the CAWVQ, they also maintained the flagrantly unfair article stipulating that a man could separate from his wife if she committed adultery, whereas a wife could not do so unless her husband "kept his concubine in the common home."

The modifications to the Civil Code were offered as a consolation prize to appease the suffragists, as they themselves were fully aware. The LWR annual report for 1931–32 observed, "Women were thrown some crumbs to content themselves with, but it remains to obtain the essential thing, suffrage." The vote therefore remained the subject of intense representations and heated debate. In addition to arguments that referred to the difference of the sexes, to equality between men and women, and to fundamental democratic principles linking citizenship and the right to vote, the suffragists and their allies highlighted the fact that though women already voted at the federal level, the institution of the family had not suffered the catastrophic collapse predicted by opponents of suffrage. In 1933, Anatole Plante dwelt more specifically on the incongruity of the fact that Quebec women were eligible for political functions everywhere except in their own province. "Our women may be Canadian delegates to Geneva for meetings of the Society of Nations, senators and members in the House of Commons in Ottawa, members of our Legislative Council, and here, in our province, they may not be even simple electors," he noted. In fact, women had become eligible for senate appointments in 1929, when the Privy Council in London ruled that they were "persons," just like men. The British North America Act, which governed senate appointments, specified only that senators must be "qualified persons." The act also applied to appointments to the Legislative Council of Quebec. Thus, thanks to the Privy Council ruling, women could now be admitted to this body.

For Quebec feminists, the exclusion of women from suffrage, like the absence of social laws that favoured them, constituted not only an injustice, but also a true shame. For instance, in March 1928, Georgina Bélanger, a Quebec feminist, journalist, and author who wrote under the name Gaétane de Montreuil, attended a speech given by Agnes Macphail, a suffragist and federal MP. In the May issue of *Mon Magazine*, Bélanger recalled, "We felt the blush of humiliation rise to our foreheads as we measured the injustice that puts us, compared to all the other provinces of the Dominion, in such an inferior state." Others, including Idola Saint-Jean, pointed out that women had acquired the vote in certain non-Western countries, such as Turkey and India. How disgraceful therefore that the women of Quebec – whose province was white, "civilized," and superior to those "Oriental" countries – did not. Saint-Jean published this opinion in the 26 February 1927 issue of *Le Monde ouvrier* and reiterated it in a series of *Montreal Herald* articles during the winter of 1930.

To this racist argument, which resembled those of some English Canadian suffragists, Saint-Jean added a measure of contempt for women who rejected the right to vote. "It is possible that in certain distant ridings, having had no contact with modern political progress, elderly women are apathetic on this question. Some may even be hostile to it," she wrote in the *Herald*. By contrast, women who were "cultivated, intelligent, progressive" were demanding the franchise. Similarly, when Anatole Plante spoke in defence of his 1932 suffrage bill, he suggested that women who opposed the vote were simply being manipulated. To add clarity, he compared them to blacks in Louisiana who had been made to believe "that freedom was an atrocious thing." Like their sisters in other provinces, many Quebec feminists also deplored that intelligent women could not express their opinion on the management of public affairs, whereas ignorant men were at liberty to do so – an argument that several members of the Legislative Assembly took up.

By pointing out that Turkish women had recently been
enfranchised, this cartoon presents the situation of their Quebec
sisters as an embarrassment. For this bemused woman, the female
citizens of a country less advanced than her own province now
held a right that was denied to her, which surely contradicted the
natural order. Some suffragists felt that industrialized nations,
as the most enlightened and progressive in the world, should
be leading the way, not lagging behind.

More rarely, but nevertheless on several occasions, the proponents of suffrage also invoked the support, or at least the neutrality, of the church. For example, William Tremblay stated in
1929, "It has been claimed that the Catholic Church was against
this right. That is absolutely false, as it has never pronounced itself against this suffrage." In 1938, Grégoire Bélanger of Montréal-
Dorion, who sponsored the suffrage bill of that year, quoted Father
Antonin-Gilbert Sertillanges at length. A French Dominican philosopher, Sertillanges felt that denying women the vote was "the
most outrageous omission of their human dignity." And feminists,
in the late 1920s at least, cited the authority of Father Alfred

LAQUELLE PRÉFÉREZ-VOUS?

Opposition to women's suffrage remained strong in Quebec until
the late 1930s. This November 1939 cartoon, published in a
student newspaper called *Le Quartier Latin,* shows that young
men shared this antagonism. Obviously, students preferred a
loving wife who put her family first rather than a pipe-smoking
Thérèse Casgrain driving a delivery truck.

Baudrillart, rector of the Institut catholique in Paris and a propon-
ent of suffrage, to bolster their demands. The attitude of these
feminists, like that of the pro-suffrage politicians, shows that if
the clergy was more discreet at the time, it nonetheless cast a long
shadow over the debates.

For their part, the adversaries of female enfranchisement were
only too happy to cite the antagonism of the Quebec clergy, who
reinforced their position and gave them a form of moral authority.
For instance, the member for Montréal-Laurier, Ernest Poulin,
said in 1933 that the "1909 Council of Quebec City disapproved of
women's suffrage, as being contrary to Christian ideas ... Should
we not listen to the voices of our religious leaders?" However, this
was neither their only argument, nor, by a long shot, their most

frequently used. As mentioned above, the idea that women did not want the vote, that it represented no more or less than a burden of which they were gallantly willing to relieve them, and that it was a threat to household peace represented some of the reasons repeated as a litany. Like Henri Bourassa in another era, they maintained that the physical differences between the sexes produced the differing aptitudes and functions of men and women – a fact that justified the denial of suffrage. Even more, they saw enfranchisement as an obstacle to motherhood and thus to French Canadian survival, as prolific mothers were necessary if the nation were to endure. "Women who have children are superior to those who are concerned with obtaining the right to vote," proclaimed Arthur Bélanger, member for Lévis, during the 1932 suffrage debate. Raoul-Paul Bachand, member for Shefford, adopted his idea during the same debate, stating that anglophone women were concerned with the vote precisely because they had fewer children. Given their views, it is hardly surprising that these men did not see the absence of suffrage as an object of shame for Quebec. To the contrary, as nationalists, they congratulated themselves on not following the path taken by their Anglo-Protestant neighbours. Instead, they kept their eyes fixed on France – where women did not vote either, as they liked to point out. For these members, being unable to vote in no way meant that women could not obtain reforms, as attested to by the amendments to the Civil Code and the access of French women to careers in the liberal professions. Others, using rather specious reasoning, stated that the heroines of New France, such as the nuns who had done missionary work among "savage or heretical peoples," had accomplished great things without having the right to vote.

Often rambling and incoherent, sometimes insulting or even frankly misogynous, the remarks of some anti-suffrage members were so arrogant, and even vulgar, that they were denounced not only by the suffragists but also, finally, by Le Devoir. On 21 January 1932, though firmly opposed to suffrage, the paper remarked that "the Chamber is not the place for crude jokes," a comment that said much about the tone of the debate in the Legislative Assembly. During that year, it must be said that these members outdid themselves. Joseph Filion offered to lend Saint-Jean his trousers whenever she wanted them. Arthur Bélanger compared female voters to "streetwalkers." And member Raoul-Paul Bachand claimed that a woman had said to him, "A Sèvres porcelain vase suits me much better than a ballot box." In the 30 January issue of *Le Monde ouvrier*, writing as Julien Saint-Michel, Éva Circé-Côté remarked that the suffrage question had "unleashed the male, as if a red rag had been waved under his snout." She found this gratifying, for "it is by flying off the handle ... that he shows his true nature." Linking this excess of profanity and aggressiveness with a pathological fear of gender role reversal, Circé-Côté nevertheless warned suffragists to resist the temptation to act as outrageously as the men – a point no doubt aimed at Saint-Jean, the favourite target of some members. For instance, in 1935, after stating, "There are too many foxes in politics to introduce hens into the mix," member Bachand once again boorishly attacked her. He borrowed from the thought of Francis Bacon, a seventeenth-century philosopher who had categorized the intellectual fallacies of human beings under four headings, which he called idols, or "idola." Bachand accurately listed them as the "*idola tribus, idola specus, idola fori,* or *idola theatri.*" Bacon's point was that error arose from several sources – human nature (tribus), individuals (specus), language (fori), and experts (theatri). Bachand's rather ponderous point was that it had just one source – Idola.

As some editorialists remarked, the arguments of anti-suffrage lawmakers were ultimately exposed for what they truly were: pretexts for not granting a right that most women were not demanding and that would interfere with the old ways of conducting politics. Although some members seemed genuinely to fear that casting a ballot would "masculinize women" or that they would take their seats in the Legislative Assembly, many opposed suffrage much more through opportunism than deep conviction. In fact, they often changed their votes from one year to the next, depending on their partisan interests or the personal advantages they might gain from sailing with the wind of the moment. Many reversed their opinion, shamelessly exploiting the issue of suffrage in an unedifying politics that was concerned far more with power plays than with democratic principles.

As the 1936 suffrage debate unfolded, the Taschereau government was rocked by numerous scandals. Feeling vulnerable, the premier decided to close ranks, so he forced all his members to vote against the bill, which had traditionally been a free vote. As instructed, Minister of Labour Edgar Rochette reversed his position, even though he had sponsored the bill of the previous year. He invoked the "fanatical, even disloyal, agitation that we must confront at the present time" – an allusion to the obstruction that Duplessis was throwing in the face of the newly re-elected Liberal government due to the corruption that had plagued the Liberals for many years. In Rochette's opinion, now was not the time for bold experiments. In fact, it would be "better, for the moment, not to complicate our electoral laws by bringing in a new element that would not contribute at all to clarifying the atmosphere." According to the 28 May *Montreal Gazette,* the Liberals feared that newly enfranchised women would be influenced by the clergy, which was hostile to their party, and would vote against it during its moment of weakness. Duplessis, who refused to take a position during the debate, felt that before admitting new voters, it would be best to "reform [the] electoral laws to purify and clean electoral house, so that women could enter a clean, accommodating place." Like elected municipal officials in the early twentieth century, he expected that many women would abstain from voting because they were not interested in politics, and he voiced his anxiety about the fraud that might ensue. This argument was less than credible, given that his Union nationale government became a by-word for underhanded tactics and corruption during the post-war period. Nonetheless, after the Liberals fell, totally discredited by the revelations of their party's extortions, the Union nationale swept to victory in the summer election of 1936, leaving women at an impasse.

Only in 1939, thanks to the intervention of Duplessis, were the suffragists invited to present their arguments before the standing committee on public bills, but it was in vain. Though the press praised the quality and solidity of their plea – *Le Devoir* expressed its admiration on the front page of its 30 March issue – the bill was once again rejected. By asking the suffragists to expound their views to the parliamentarians before the bill was debated, was Duplessis seeking to make their failure even more crushing? It is difficult to understand his strategy, but it must be said that he had previously suggested, without success, that feminists should be granted a hearing. The exercise left them feeling frustrated, but they had in their pocket the promise of the Liberal Party to en-franchise them if it won the next election, which it did that fall.

Obviously, the Liberal victory was of great concern to the op-ponents of female enfranchisement. On 7 March 1940, even be-fore the suffrage bill of that year was tabled, *Le Devoir* proposed that a referendum be held among Quebec women to discover whether they wanted the vote (the paper was convinced that most would say no). The referendum never took place. In fact, British Columbia was the only Canadian province to organize a similar consultation. Held in 1916, the BC referendum asked male voters whether they favoured women's suffrage. More than two-thirds did, so it was granted the following year. On 11 April 1940, despite an intervention by Cardinal Villeneuve, who expressed his dis-agreement on behalf of all bishops in Quebec, the fourteenth suf-frage bill was introduced to the assembly. It was tabled by the new Liberal premier, Adélard Godbout, who had voted against en-franchisement in the past. The statute was adopted on 18 April 1940 and given assent on 25 April. To the end, certain members of the assembly and of the Legislative Council voiced their dissent

REALLY, THIS IS SO SUDDEN

A *Toronto Star* cartoon spoofs the Quebec government's lengthy delay in granting women the provincial franchise. "Quebec women" has waited so long for her timid beau to pop the question that spiders have anchored their webs to her outstretched arm. Even the god of love, dozing on the mantelpiece after fruitlessly emptying his quiver, has not succeeded in hurrying things along. Despite the playfulness of this image, women were added to the provincial electorate only after a long and fierce struggle.

by singing the old song of separate spheres and the mother as guardian of the home. At the dawn of a world war, during which women's support and contributions would be essential, this rearguard defence seemed completely disconnected from reality.

⌘

More than twenty years after the majority of Canadian, American, and British women, Quebec women of European ancestry finally obtained the right to vote. They won the battle a few years before

French and Belgian women, so they were not completely out of sync with the West overall, particularly the Catholic countries. As researcher Sylvie D'Augerot-Arend and, more recently, historian Alexandre Dumas note, opposition from the Catholic Church was not solely responsible for this delay. Indeed, it was grounded in a combination of issues. That politicians, many of them profoundly conservative or even openly misogynistic, did not see how suffrage could be of use to women – a view shared by many women outside of Montreal – was one major contributing factor. Based essentially on the idea of preserving the gender identities within which the national identity of French Canadians was embodied, this opposition would decline at the advent of the war, which considerably changed the political power plays.

In fact, the persistent underrepresentation of women in the political world was, in some ways, an extension of the era when they had been excluded from that world. Moving toward better representation of women would thus help to reverse this situation.

– DIRECTEUR GÉNÉRAL DES ÉLECTIONS DU QUÉBEC,
FEMMES ET POLITIQUE: FACTEURS D'INFLUENCE,
MESURES INCITATIVES ET EXPOSÉ DE LA
SITUATION QUÉBÉCOISE, 2014

FIVE

REACHING FOR REPRESENTATION

Standing before the National Assembly of Quebec, this monument to female politicians was inaugurated on 5 December 2012. Grouped at the left are Marie Lacoste Gérin-Lajoie, Idola Saint-Jean, and Thérèse Casgrain, who fought for suffrage in the early twentieth century. Marie-Claire Kirkland-Casgrain, the first woman elected to the assembly, stands at the right, set apart from the others to mark the gap in time between the two events.

BETWEEN THE FIRST and Second World Wars, the suffragists fought tirelessly to win their battle. Their victory in 1940 was not complete, however, because "registered Indians" – Indigenous people who held Indian status under the law – still could not vote in provincial or federal elections. Nor could the Inuit. People of Asian origin were also excluded federally and in British Columbia and Saskatchewan. These last obstacles to recognition of their political citizenship were lifted only in 1948. Nor did the suffragist victory mark the end of all battles on the political front. Rather, the struggle moved from enfranchisement to representation. Quebec women first voted provincially in 1944, but no woman was elected to the assembly until 1961, more than fifteen years later. And another twenty years would elapse before the assembly boasted more than six female members. Obviously, these dismally low numbers, especially in cabinets, were a concern for feminists. They remain so today, as feminists are being called upon to address the ways in which women achieve and exercise power and to deal with nationalist revivals or awakenings in various communities, both white and Indigenous.

INDIGENOUS WOMEN

Until 1960, members of First Nations who lived on-reserve could not vote federally unless they were "emancipated." That is, they renounced their ancestral or treaty rights and the status conferred upon them by the Indian Act, which dated from the nineteenth century. As set out by the statute, the emancipation process required them to prove that they had sufficient knowledge of

English or French, that they had received an elementary education, and that they were "of good character" and free of debt. In
other words, they had to demonstrate that they had acquired the
skills and assimilated the values of the white population – even if
whites themselves were far from possessing these qualities – and
had surrendered not only their rights but their Indigenous identity. Given all this, it is not surprising that few opted for emancipation. In response to their resistance, Ottawa even emancipated
some Indigenous people without their consent, including university graduates, First World War veterans, and women who married
white men. Until 1985, these women automatically lost their
Indian status.

In 1960, Ottawa enfranchised all status Indians, granting
them the right to vote under the same conditions as the white
population, even though Indigenous people had not expressly
demanded that it do so. Twelve years earlier, in 1948, a parliamentary committee had recommended that Ottawa phase out its
administrative supervision of the First Nations, and Canada had
adopted the Canadian Bill of Rights, which recognized the formal equality of all citizens. Therefore, the enfranchisement of
all Indigenous people, without restrictions, seemed unavoidable.
However, the legacy of colonialism did not encourage high voter
turnout among Indigenous people. This was especially true in
Quebec, where, according to some calculations, barely 35 percent
of on-reserve registered voters cast a ballot in the 2000 federal
election. In reality, acquiring the vote had never been a major concern for Indigenous people. Long synonymous with assimilation,
it was not seen as a means of significantly improving their situation and living conditions. Rather than turning to the vote, the
Indigenous movement that sprang up in the 1960s focused on the
treaties that had been concluded with the white government.
Demanding that the treaties be honoured, it campaigned for more
autonomy and for the preservation of First Nations culture and
ways of life. Like nationalist movements in white society, it

stressed the transmission of ancestral customs by women, which sometimes caused tension between them and male leaders.

The situation of the Inuit was very different. Before Confederation, they simply could not vote, as they lived on land that the Hudson's Bay Company controlled, not in the territory that would become Canada in 1867. In 1950, they were granted the federal franchise, but polling places were not made available to them, so they could not exercise this right. The situation was corrected only in 1962. In Quebec, Indigenous people who lived on reserves were formally deprived of the vote in the 1915 provincial election and did not recover it until 1969. During the debate in the assembly over the bill that would return this right, Jean-Jacques Bertrand, the minister responsible for this portfolio, observed that Indigenous people who did not live on-reserve had always possessed it, at least in theory. Citing the Inuit and the James Bay Cree, he pointed out that it was illusory, as their "territories of Nouveau-Québec and Mistassini are not part of any riding." This would soon change, but Indigenous people did not rush to the polls in large numbers.

Although Indigenous people did not obtain federal and provincial enfranchisement until recently, and Quebec was the last province to grant them the vote, the Indian Act of 1876 recognized their right to elect band councils to manage their local affairs. The councils, however, came under the supervision of Ottawa, which reserved the right to oversee the administration of communities. As a result, elected band council members had limited decision-making power. What is more, council elections were patterned after white norms and took no account of Indigenous political traditions. Nor did they recognize the ancestral systems of government in which women could take an active role, as mentioned in Chapter 1. In the opinion of the colonizers, Indigenous social organization, and women's place within it, simply reflected the primitive nature of these peoples. Therefore, they sought to impose their own patriarchal norm to ensure that men dominated women – attempts that were systematized by the Indian Act of 1876. In 1951, the act was revised. As a result, more than thirty years after most Canadian women acquired the federal franchise, Indigenous women were permitted to vote and to run for office in band council elections. In Quebec, Violet Pachano, of the Cree community of Chisasibi, was the first woman to be elected to a band council, in the 1980s. In 2015, the *Gazette des femmes* estimated that women made up about 34 percent of the forty band councils in Quebec. Four of them were chiefs. Two councils, those of Mingan and La Romaine, had opted for parity – equally dividing their membership between men and women. In Nunavik, women accounted for 43 percent of the elected representatives in the fourteen village councils, and three were mayors. As we shall see, these data compare advantageously with those for women elected in all Quebec municipalities and in the National Assembly (the Legislative Assembly became the National Assembly in 1968). Like them, Indigenous and Inuit women are responsible mainly for portfolios of a social nature – health, welfare, education, and family, especially conjugal violence – an aspect of women in politics that seems to cross ethnic or racial borders and that will be discussed below. It is worth noting that in the fall of 2016, Éva Ottawa, an Attikamek who was the first woman to lead her nation's council, was appointed chair of the Conseil du statut de la femme, a government advisory body on issues regarding women's status, setting another precedent. Several months earlier, numerous Algonquin women from the Val-d'Or region had denounced the abuses committed by officers of the Sûreté du Québec (the provincial police). Viviane Michel, president of Femmes autochtones du Québec, felt that Ottawa's appointment offered a unique opportunity for First Nations women to make themselves heard. Unfortunately, Ottawa resigned in late January 2017, explaining simply, according to the 2 February

issue of *La Presse*, that her priority had always been "the fate reserved for Indigenous women." In other words, unlike Viviane
Michel, Ottawa was not convinced that her position could allow
her to effectively defend their claims and bring forward their
preoccupations.

Even before they could be elected to band councils, Indigenous
women were committed to their Canada-wide struggle against a
clause in the Indian Act that deprived them of their Indian status

MARY TWO-AXE EARLEY
(1911–96)

*Born in Kahnawake to a Mohawk father (Dominic Onenhariio)
and an Oneida mother (Juliet Smith), Mary Two-Axe moved to
the United States with her mother when her parents separated.
When her mother died, in 1919, she returned to Canada to
live with her paternal grandparents. She spent her adult life in
Brooklyn, New York, where she married an Irishman, Edward
Earley, with whom she had two children, but she returned
regularly with her family to vacation on the reserve where she
was born. In 1966, she became aware of the broad range of re-
percussions that affected Indigenous women who married out.
A Mohawk friend had done so and had been forced to leave
her reserve as a result. When she died of a heart attack, Two-
Axe Earley was convinced that the stress of her eviction was
responsible. Thus, she initiated the struggle to end this form of
discrimination in the Indian Act. At the suggestion of Thérèse
Casgrain, she and thirty other Mohawk women submitted a
brief to the Royal Commission on the Status of Women (the*

should they marry a white man. (Indigenous men who married white women did not lose their status.) This battle, initiated in the 1960s by a Mohawk woman named Mary Two-Axe Earley, lasted more than twenty-five years. Born on the Kahnawake reserve, she founded Equal Rights for Native Women specifically for this purpose. Any Indigenous woman who married out was evicted from her community of birth, dispossessed of any property she might own there, and prevented from participating in

Bird Commission) to denounce this injustice. To expand the scope of the struggle, she founded the Quebec organization Equal Rights for Native Women in 1968. Its counterpart in English Canada, Indian Rights for Indian Women, was created in 1973. When her husband died in 1969, she returned to the reserve to live in the house that her grandparents had left her, but she ran into resistance from the band council, which only tolerated her presence. Its opposition continued even though, in 1971, she transferred ownership of the house to her daughter, who had married a Mohawk. In 1975, while she was in Mexico City attending an international conference on the status of women, Two-Axe Earley learned that the band council had decided to expel her. Taking advantage of the platform offered by the conference, she denounced the situation of First Nations women in Canada and pled their cause, but it took another ten years of struggle before the Indian Act was finally amended.

Mary Two-Axe Earley instigated the fight by Indigenous women to abolish discriminatory clauses in the Indian Act. She is seen here in 1983, two years before some of their demands were met.

its political life and accessing its services. She even lost her right to be buried there. This was the case for Two-Axe Earley and for one of her Mohawk friends, Lucie Lovelace.

Tabled in 1970, the report of the Bird Commission recommended that the Indian Act be amended "to allow an Indian woman upon marriage to a non-Indian to (a) retain her Indian status and (b) transmit her Indian status to her children." These recommendations were met with fierce opposition from Indigenous leaders, who feared that whites would thus become majorities in reserves, grab the meagre resources conferred by the state, and favour the assimilation of Indigenous people. In other words, the nationalism that fed the affirmation of Indigenous people entered into direct conflict with the equally legitimate demands of Indigenous women. A relentless struggle began, as the women held public demonstrations and made representations to political and legal bodies, including the human rights committee of the United Nations. Eventually, they took their case to the Supreme Court of Canada, which decided against them in 1973. In 1985, three years after the adoption of the Canadian Charter of Rights and Freedoms, they gained a partial victory. Bill C-31, which recognized the principle of equality between men and women, modified the Indian Act. Now, Indigenous women who had married out, as well as the children of that union, could recover their status. When the Gender Equity in Indian Registration Act was passed in 2011, this disposition was finally extended to the women's grandchildren, even if they did not marry an Indigenous man.

Nonetheless, the triumph was not complete. Ottawa had delegated application of the law to the various band councils, some of which refused to reintegrate women who had married white men or to register their children. They cited insufficient resources as their reason. As anthropologist Audra Simpson observes, Indigenous people feared that the change to the Indian Act would pave the way for whites to seize parts of their territory. They also saw it as a denial of their authority over their own lands. Simpson notes that in 1981, the Kahnawake band council had adopted a recommendation that withdrew all rights and privileges from Kahnawake Mohawks who married non-Indians. These included the right to live on-reserve, to own property there, and to vote and run for office in band council elections. As justification for this move, the council referred to the Indian Act. In 1984, the council adopted another measure, which specified that people who were born after that year must have at least 50 percent Indian blood to be considered members of the band. These types of policies, which affected both men and women, sparked much debate in the community because they conflicted with other ideas about how one belonged to the Mohawk Nation, including affiliation with a clan mother. Although most Mohawk leaders felt that Ottawa had no business deciding who qualified as an Indian or who could live on-reserve, some also contested the authority of the band council, which had been established by the white government. In their view, permitting the council to determine who could live among Indigenous people amounted to relying on a white institution to defend Indigenous traditions, which was unacceptable.

Mohawk women shared the nationalist preoccupations of their leaders. They too felt that their people should exercise self-determination and that their culture, language, and way of life should be protected. However, they drew the line at discriminatory practices that targeted them or other members of the community. On her Facebook page, quoted in *La Presse* on 15 August 2014, Ellen Gabriel, a leading figure among the Indigenous women of Quebec, noted that the band council's 50 percent rule "does not arise from any Mohawk law, but derives from the colonial assimilation instituted by the *Indian Act.*" Indigenous values are incompatible with the search for "racial purity," Gabriel added, because it contradicts the tradition of adopting strangers and integrating them into the clan. As the Mohawk author Patricia Monture-Angus wrote in her book *Thunder in My Soul,* "Many of the rules developed to protect Indians are now used by Indians against Indians, particularly against Indian women. This is an indication that the colonized have accepted their colonization. As a result of the internalization of colonization, the colonizers can step back from the devastation caused by their acts."

The Association des femmes autochtones du Québec (AFAQ), which took over from Equal Rights for Native Women in 1974, was on the front line of the battle to amend the Indian Act, and during the 1980s it was central to the struggles against the endemic scourge of family violence on reserves. The greater presence of Indigenous women on band councils and northern village councils since the 1980s has also helped to put the major issue of family violence in the spotlight. As many of those involved have observed, this problem is political because violence is usually the consequence of colonialism, which devalued – and even tried to eradicate – Indigenous culture, ways of life, traditions, and beliefs. It deconstructed families and communities, notably by the establishment of the residential school system, which removed Indigenous children from their parents and attempted to acculturate them. In its 2015 report *Honouring the Truth, Reconciling for the Future,* the Truth and Reconciliation Commission of Canada demonstrated conclusively that the emotional and sexual abuse suffered by children at these schools has left indelible traces that feed the current violence. "The impacts of the legacy of residential schools have not ended with those who attended the schools," the commission concluded. "They affected the Survivors' partners, their children, their grandchildren, their extended families, and their communities." The effects of the residential schools also extended beyond the reserves. The commission suggested that "a devastating link" probably existed "between the large numbers of missing and murdered Aboriginal women and the many harmful background factors in their lives." Even though this problem has been notorious for many years, only in December 2015 did Justin Trudeau's government create a national commission of inquiry to investigate it. Michelle Audette, an Innu activist who had led the Native Women's Association of Canada, was one of the five commissioners appointed. Despite requests from a number of organizations, including not only the AFAQ but the Assembly of First Nations Quebec-Labrador and its leader, Ghislain Picard, the Quebec government has refused to initiate a similar process.

One way to attenuate the worst effects of colonialism involves the territorial claims of Indigenous people. These aim to preserve traditional hunting and fishing practices, to improve the economic and social situation of communities, and to return a measure of autonomy to them. Over the years, Indigenous women have fully supported these claims by participating in, or even initiating or leading, acts of resistance, occupations, and blockades. For example, in 1990, the municipality of Oka scheduled the expansion of a golf course and the construction of a housing development at the Pines, an area that had long been claimed by the Mohawks of Kanehsatake as part of their ancestral territory. In March 1990, the Mohawks set up a barricade, initially symbolic, to block access to the site and halt its development. Women were prominent among those who maintained the barricade. Eventually the police and then the army were called in, and the situation deteriorated into an armed conflict. Using her Mohawk name Katsitsakwas, Ellen Gabriel was chosen as spokesperson for the traditionalists of the Longhouse to negotiate with the Quebec authorities and to present the Mohawk view to the media. The website Women Suffrage and Beyond notes that Gabriel was a central figure in this historic clash between white and Indigenous society, as much as – and perhaps more than – the warriors and Canadian soldiers who confronted each other. In September, after a standoff of seventy-eight days, the barricade was finally dismantled.

Although they support the demands of their communities, Indigenous women have nevertheless learned to be vigilant with regard to territorial claims. The same holds true for the development activities in which the Quebec government has sought to involve Indigenous people over the years. Experience has taught them that these projects, which the men in their communities may see as beneficial, do not necessarily diminish women's problems or improve their living conditions. For instance, in 2011, when the Quebec government announced an economic development program in northern Quebec, Le Plan Nord, women had to fight simply to gain a place at the discussion table. Although the state consulted the Assembly of First Nations and the band councils, it initially ignored the AFAQ, whose view differed from that of the male Indigenous leaders. As Michelle Audette, then president of the AFAQ, observed during a 2012 meeting, not all Indigenous communities agreed with Le Plan Nord. And like the government, those who endorsed it had not considered "the place of women in this societal project." She pointed out, "The jobs that result from Le Plan Nord are aimed mainly at Quebec men, then at a few Indigenous men."

During the winter of 2012, the AFAQ was finally included in the negotiations between the First Nations and the Quebec government, but this has not guaranteed that women will profit from the economic benefits of the plan. The jobs that it generates in the energy, mining, forestry, tourism, and wildlife sectors are traditionally held by men. The office jobs that support these operations, and that usually go to women, are located to the south, far out of reach for the Indigenous women of northern Quebec. In the view of Évelyne Roy, a researcher who has studied the question, "Band councils have internalized the sexist attitudes of the colonizers and do not consider in their debates the problems experienced by women." Thus, women cannot count on the councils to defend their interests. As Roy notes, when band councils receive large sums of money from the state, they tend not to think of devoting some of it to resolving conjugal violence, opening daycare centres, or training women workers. Just as they had to fight to preserve their Indian status when they married out, Indigenous women must now fight to obtain their share of the available money, thus confirming that they are members of the Indigenous nations that receive this money.

In 2009, the Working Group of Elected Women of the Assembly of First Nations Quebec-Labrador and the Conseil du statut de la femme jointly conducted a study among elected Indigenous women. They consulted twenty-two women, almost all of whom agreed that parity between men and women in political institutions was a priority that would "ensure balance in decision-making processes." Many deplored that women who wished to be involved in politics were encountering ever greater obstacles. They were also dismayed that women were often appointed to portfolios of a family or social nature, whereas those involving territorial claims or territorial development remained the bailiwick of men. This trend helped to ensure that women's views would not necessarily be taken into account when the fate of a community was decided. As we shall see below, white female politicians experienced similar realities. They too called for the imposition of parity, believing that it would resolve the democratic deficit resulting from the low representation of women in parliamentary politics.

WOMEN IN POLITICS

In the 1940s, while she was conducting research for her doctoral dissertation on the history of women's suffrage in Canada, Catherine Cleverdon contacted a number of suffragists in English Canada and Quebec. She asked them various questions, including this one, reproduced in a letter to Thérèse Casgrain on 31 August 1946: "Do you think Canadian women have evinced or are evincing any serious interest in political questions and activities?" According to several women who replied to her letters, including Grace Ritchie-England, Casgrain, and Constance P. Garneau, the new president of the League for Women's Rights, Canadian women, especially Quebec women, were not generally very enthusiastic about politics. A few, most of them anglophones, were becoming increasingly interested, but the others showed an indifference that the correspondents imputed to ignorance and old prejudices. "There are groups that still think that it is unladylike if not vaguely immoral for women to be interested in politics," observed Garneau in her response of 26 September. According to Ritchie-England, the fact that the platforms of the major political parties were so similar did little to pique the interest of women. And if female candidates were not legion, it was because they were often relegated to ridings that they had no chance of winning. Money was an obstacle as well. Electoral expenses, especially the deposit that they risked losing if they did not garner

WOMEN EXERCISE FRANCHISE FOR FIRST TIME

Women exercised their franchise in the Province of Quebec for the first time yesterday, and under the stress of wartime conditions, had to make special arrangements to do it. In this group, shown in Poll 85, Outremont Division, are a number who parked their youngsters with friends while they voted, and who later took care of friends' youngsters to allow them a similar opportunity.

On 8 August 1944, the majority of Quebec women participated in a provincial election for the first time. Although they had voted federally since 1921, a *Montreal Gazette* photographer visited a polling station in Outremont to immortalize the historic moment.

enough votes, were too onerous for their limited financial means. As Ritchie-England emphasized in her 23 September letter, men could draw professional advantages from their candidacy, even if they did not win their seat, because it heightened their visibility in the community. Furthermore, the political parties might find them jobs within their organizations. In short, according to Ritchie-England's analysis, which resembled that of contemporary political scientists, women who competed in the race for office encountered more obstacles than did men and did not benefit at all. Therefore, they were not much encouraged to enter politics.

Nevertheless, a few women did try to get elected during the 1940s and 1950s. This was not a first, as Ritchie-England and Idola Saint-Jean had preceded them in the 1930 federal election, though neither won her riding. Ritchie-England was the official candidate for the Liberal Party in the riding of Mount Royal, and Saint-Jean

"Le bonheur du peuple dépend d'un bon Gouvernement"

IDOLA SAINT-JEAN
Candidate Libérale Indépendante
pour la division Saint-Denis

BULLETIN DE VOTE

DR. J. A. DENIS	
J. C. GAUTHIER	
IDOLA SAINT-JEAN	**X**

MARQUEZ VOTRE BULLETIN POUR MELLE SAINT-JEAN

Idola Saint-Jean's election campaign poster of 1930 links the well-being of the people with good government, though it makes no specific promises. Running as an independent Liberal candidate (that is, without support from the Liberal Party), she lost the election, though she garnered a respectable number of votes.

was an independent Liberal candidate in Montréal-Dorion-Saint-Denis. Because Saint-Jean ran as an independent, she received no support from the party, unlike Ritchie-England. According to data gathered by political scientist Manon Tremblay in *Québécoises et représentation parlementaire,* the number of Quebec female candidates did not exceed ten until the 1953 federal election. None were elected that year. In 1972, their number jumped to twenty-nine from just nine in 1968. The 1972 election also marked Quebec women's entry into the House of Commons, as Monique Bégin, Albanie Morin, and Jeanne Sauvé, all Liberals, won their seats. Bégin, who had been secretary of the Bird Commission in the 1960s, was an unabashed feminist, which was not necessarily true of Morin or Sauvé. However, Sauvé said that she was proud to have opened the first daycare centre on Parliament Hill. She was also chosen as Speaker of the House of Commons in 1980 and as governor general in 1983, two firsts. According to the Library and Archives Canada website, she described these appointments as "a magnificent breakthrough for women." She always refused to have the French versions of these titles feminized, though, because in her view they designated the position, not the person who occupied it.

Marie-Claire Kirkland-Casgrain was the first woman to sit in the Legislative Assembly of Quebec, following a 1961 by-election in the riding of Jacques-Cartier. She was not, however, the first woman to run for provincial office in Quebec. She was preceded by Mae Leehy O'Connor, who was defeated in a 1947 by-election in the riding of Huntingdon. It is notable that both ran for the Liberal Party and that the member whom they hoped to replace had died in office and was related to them. In the case of Leehy O'Connor, this was her husband; for Kirkland-Casgrain, it was her father. Thus, the two women campaigned not solely on their own merits but also as "wife of" or "daughter of." This strategy was not unique. Mary Ellen Smith of British Columbia and Martha Black of the Yukon had both employed it, and successfully. When Smith's husband died, she won the resulting by-election of 1918, running as an independent and becoming the first woman elected to the British Columbia legislature. Later, she ran as a Liberal and was also the first woman to be appointed a cabinet minister in the entire British Empire. Martha Black, the second woman elected to the Parliament of Canada, ran for the Conservatives in 1935,

Marie-Claire Kirkland-Casgrain walks with a determined step
among a group of male politicians, including Montreal mayor
Jean Drapeau, to her immediate right. The first woman elected to
the Legislative Assembly, in 1961, she remained its only female
representative throughout the 1960s.

taking over from her husband, who was unable to continue due to
health problems.

According to the data compiled by Manon Tremblay and those
available on the website of the Directeur général des élections du
Québec, two, three, and seven women ran unsuccessfully in the
provincial general elections of 1948, 1952, and 1956. Among them
was Thérèse Casgrain, who initially represented the Co-operative
Commonwealth Federation, which became the Parti social démocratique. Almost all the others ran for the Labor-Progressive Party,
which replaced the Communist Party when it was banned in 1941.
Therefore, until the 1960s, if they were not seeking to replace a deceased relative, female candidates stood for marginal left-wing
parties that had no chance of winning. Their numbers did not rise
above twenty until the 1973 general election. By then, most were

MARIE-CLAIRE KIRKLAND-CASGRAIN
(1924–2016)

Born in the United States, Marie-Claire Kirkland was the daughter of a physician. After she became a lawyer in 1952, she was a founding member of the Association des femmes avocates de la province de Québec. She was active in the Liberal Party, first as a consultant for the Young Liberals in her riding, then as president of the Fédération des femmes libérales du Québec. Her father, a long-time Liberal and member of the Legislative Assembly, had represented the riding of Jacques-Cartier from 1939 to his death in the summer of 1961. When he died, she seemed the ideal choice to run for his vacant seat. In fact, she easily won the by-election of 14 December 1961, becoming the first woman to be elected to the Quebec Legislative Assembly. Re-elected the following year in the general election, she became a minister without portfolio and shepherded Bill 16 through the legislative process. This important statute ended the legal incapacity of married women. Before it came into effect, a wife could not take legal action without her husband's signature. Thus, as she liked to recount, Kirkland-Casgrain needed her husband to sign the lease for the Quebec City apartment that she rented during parliamentary sessions. Re-elected in 1966 in the same riding, now called Marguerite-Bourgeoys at her suggestion, she succeeded in having a law adopted that made partnership of acquests, which made both spouses responsible for management of the family properties, the legal matrimonial regime, even though the Liberals were the official Opposition at the time. During her final mandate, from 1970 to 1973, she presided over the creation of the Conseil du statut de la femme. She then left politics to be a judge on the Provincial Court and president of the Minimum Wage Commission. She ended her career on the bench in the judicial district of Montreal.

Thérèse Casgrain ran for federal or provincial office at least seven
times between 1942 and 1963, first as an independent Liberal and
then for the Parti social démocratique, the French name for the
Co-operative Commonwealth Federation, which became the
New Democratic Party in 1961. Here, she is seen during a federal
election of the 1950s, when she ran in the Montreal riding of
Jacques-Cartier–Lasalle.

representing a mainstream party: two for the Liberals, seven for
the Parti québécois, and nine for the Union nationale. Just one,
Liberal Lise Bacon, won her seat. Only in the 1981 election did the
proportion of female candidates, all parties combined, reach 15
percent. In 2007, the proportion stood at just over 31 percent, a
peak that was surpassed only in 2018, when women comprised
47.2 percent of the candidates. It should be added that in September 2012, Pauline Marois, who had led the Parti québécois for
five years, became the province's first female premier. Her minority government lost the early election of April 2014, barely eight-
een months after she was sworn in, which prompted her
retirement from political life. Today, only Manon Massé, who succeeded Françoise David as co-spokesperson of Québec solidaire,
retains a leadership position in a Quebec political party.

PAULINE MAROIS
(1949–)

A social worker by training, Pauline Marois began her political career in 1978 as press attaché for Jacques Parizeau, the Quebec minister of finance. In 1979, she became chief of staff for Lise Payette, minister of state for status of women, a portfolio that she herself took over after she was elected for the Parti québécois in the riding of La Peltrie in 1981. Until she was defeated in the 1985 election, she occupied a variety of positions, sometimes concurrently: vice-chair of the Treasury Board (1982–85), vice-minister of status of women (1982–83), and minister of labour and income security (1983–85). Re-elected constantly from 1989 to 2006, she headed the most important government departments in the Parizeau, Bouchard, and Landry cabinets, including Health and Social Services; Education; Child and Family Welfare; Administration and Civil Service; Treasury Board; Finance and Revenue; Research, Science, and Technology; and Industry and Trade. From 2001 to 2003, she was also vice-premier. The importance of these positions and the vast experience that she accumulated were not enough, however, to get her elected party leader in 2005. In 2007, after her predecessor resigned, she became the first woman to occupy the position. Leader of the Opposition from 2008 to 2012, she was the first woman, in September 2012, to become premier. She left politics in 2014, after the Parti québécois lost the election and she was defeated in her own riding.

It was also during the 1940s that women made a first breakthrough in municipal politics. In the early 1930s, thanks to pressure from various women's associations, wives who owned property had finally obtained the right to vote in Montreal elections. Ten years later, three women sat on the council. They were

FRANÇOISE DAVID
(1948–)

Françoise David, who has a bachelor's degree in social work, entered politics in the 2000s, following several decades of activism in various community and feminist groups. After working as a community organizer, she became the co-ordinator of the Regroupement des centres de femmes du Québec (1987–94) and was then president of the Fédération des femmes du Québec (1994–2001). On behalf of the federation, she organized the Marche des femmes contre la pauvreté, also known as the Women's March for Bread and Roses (1995), and the World March of Women against Poverty and Violence (2000). In 2004, she helped to found the Option citoyenne movement, and she signed the Manifeste pour un Québec solidaire *in 2005. This was a rebuttal to the* Manifeste pour un Québec lucide, *which was published by right-wing personalities at the instigation of former Quebec premier Lucien Bouchard. The* Manifeste pour un Québec solidaire *advocated for more social justice and solidarity among Quebecers. The* Manifeste pour un Québec lucide *described a major demographic, economic, and financial crisis and demanded that radical changes be made to the economic and social functioning of Quebec to solve the problem. Its authors recommended deep cuts to social*

Lucie Lamoureux-Bruneau, co-founder of Hôpital Sainte-Justine pour enfants and of several organizations for people with disabilities, Jessie Kathleen Fisher (Grace Ritchie-England's niece), and Elizabeth Monk, both of whom were active in the League for Women's Rights. Although a few women held the position of

programs and to protection of the most vulnerable populations. In the following year, Québec solidaire, born of the merger of Option citoyenne and the Union des forces progressistes, officially became a political party. David was elected its co-spokesperson. After two failed tries in 2007 and 2008, she was elected to the National Assembly in 2012, representing this resolutely left-wing party in the riding of Gouin. Her family has been engaged in politics for four generations. Her father, cardiologist Paul David, was a senator. Her grandfather, Athanase David, who favoured women's suffrage, was provincial secretary from 1919 to 1935 in the Louis-Alexandre Taschereau government. And her great-grandfather, Laurent-Olivier David, was a member of the Legislative Assembly in the government of Honoré Mercier, between 1886 and 1890, and then a senator. In April 2014, David's sister Hélène joined her in the assembly, having been elected for the Liberals in the Outremont riding. This marked the first instance in which two sisters sat in the legislature at the same time. In January 2017, David resigned her position as co-spokesperson and her seat in the assembly for health reasons.

deputy mayor over the years, Montreal's first female mayor was not elected until 2017. This was Valérie Plante, leader of the left-wing municipal party Projet Montréal. The first woman to win a Quebec mayoral race was probably Elsie M. Gibbons, who served from 1953 to 1971 in Portage-du-Fort, a village in the Outaouais region. Andrée P. Boucher, mayor of Sainte-Foy between 1985 and 2001, and then of Quebec City from 2005 until her sudden death in 2007, was also the first woman to lead a municipal political party. Caroline Saint-Hilaire was mayor of Longueil, the fifth-largest city in the province, from 2009 to 2017, when Sylvie Parent succeeded her. According to an inquiry conducted by the Conseil du statut de la femme in the early 2010s, 16 percent of Quebec's mayors and almost 30 percent of its councillors were women, the latter proportion more or less matching that of women sitting in the National Assembly.

As we can see, obtaining the rights to vote and to run for office did not result immediately in throngs of women entering the halls of power. In fact, only in the 1980s, and more so during the 1990s and 2000s, did the number of women in office really take off. It was not until the election of 1 October 2018 that the proportion of women in the National Assembly rose to slightly above 40 percent (42.4 percent) – a figure that many view as the bottom threshold for achievement of parity. And yet, as researchers note, it cannot be said that voters, whether male or female, systematically refuse to support female candidates, as their success rate is similar to that of men. In other words, the proportion of women elected in relation to those who run is about the same as that for men in relation to all male candidates. It is therefore prior to elections, when candidates are chosen, that the problem arises.

Several factors hinder the election of female candidates, starting with the unwillingness of women themselves to solicit the support of a political party. Lacking confidence in their ability to win the race and persuaded that they are poorly prepared for office, women, more than men, feel that they do not have the necessary qualities to represent a party and, eventually, the population. To these causes, which spring from their socialization, is added the difficulty of reconciling politics and family. Responsibility for the children and housework still falls largely to women, despite the progress made in sharing these tasks with spouses. However, the biggest barrier is the reluctance of political parties to field female candidates. As far back as 1970, the report of the Bird Commission noted that, for women, "winning the nomination is a more formidable hurdle than winning the election." This situation has changed very slowly. As mentioned, women represented a record high of 40 percent of all candidates during the October 2018 election. To explain why it took so long to attain the bottom threshold of parity, one must look above all else at the influence of the local political elite. In their search for candidates, they commonly choose people who correspond to a masculine profile, particularly in terms of education and career. Nor can women count on the same types of networks as do men, whether within political parties or in civil society, and this too is a disadvantage when they seek nomination.

In the late 1990s, the low numbers of women on municipal councils and in parliaments led to the formation of groups, such as Féminisme et démocratie, that encourage women to engage in politics through organizations financed by the government program À égalité pour décider. This strategy has serious limitations, however. As political scientist Chantal Maillé observes in a 2011 *Bulletin d'histoire politique* article, it perceives women's lack of preparation as the source of the problem and proposes its resolution as a cure-all. Rejecting this as the shaming of women, some researchers and observers of the political scene suggest that mandatory candidacy quotas must be imposed on the parties until parity is reached. Such measures have been in force in Sweden since the mid-1980s and in France since the 2000s, with the objective of having the proportion of elected men and women oscillate between 40 and 60 percent to produce real gender diversity, if not true equality. Significantly, during its August 2016 convention, the Commission jeunesse of the Quebec Liberal Party rejected a resolution of this type. According to the 14 August issue of *La Presse,* many young male activists took the floor to oppose the measure, asserting that competency should trump gender in the choice of candidates. This argument is unconvincing, however, as nothing indicates that the women chosen would be incompetent or that all male candidates are necessarily more competent.

The stance of these young Liberals shows that, until very recently, parity was a highly sensitive issue, even among the new generation of politicians. But it must also be added that on 8 March 2017, International Women's Day, a group of female ex-parliamentarians demanded that a statute be created in which the parties were forced to run a minimum of 40 percent female candidates in general elections. No law was adopted, but the pressure exerted by these women and other feminist groups did have an effect: in the October 2018 election, 47.2 percent of the candidates of the four major political parties were female (compared to 40.0 percent for all parties combined); 53 of the 125 members elected were women – an unprecedented number (and proportion, 42.4 percent). Nevertheless, the question of parity led to bitter debates throughout the first two decades of the twenty-first century and continues to be a concern for many. Some feel that the disproportionately low number of women in politics is a real democratic deficit that must be redressed, by coercion if necessary. For them, the imposition of parity is an ideal way to ensure better representation of women and their concerns. Others dismiss it as simply unacceptable. In their view, parity is anti-democratic because it presumes that women can represent only their own group, whereas that group is far from homogeneous, as women do not share the same interests or support the same ideas. Furthermore, according to political scientist Eleni Varikas, parity condones the idea of the difference between the sexes and would thus merely perpetuate the domination of women, which thrives on this differentiation. On their own, technical solutions such as quotas cannot reverse the subjugation of women. In a book published in 2015, Quebec journalist and essayist Pascale Navarro presents a contrary view. She maintains that parity could only benefit society, as more equitable participation of women in power would encourage the consideration of concerns that are particularly important to them. Without claiming that women form a monolithic bloc and necessarily share the same view on all questions, Navarro argues that real sexual diversity would broaden the spectrum of debates. She suggests that women's experience and socialization, not just their biology, cause them to look at the world differently than men do. Furthermore, parity would simply reflect the demographic composition of the population.

In the debates around parity, the question of difference versus equality of the sexes has therefore resurfaced. Like the feminists in the early twentieth century, who claimed that the maternal capacities of women justified awarding them the vote, those who militate in favour of quotas feel that women are shaped by their daily experience, which differs from that of men. A truly democratic society must take this into account by promoting female representation in the political arena. In her book *Parité!* American political historian Joan Scott dissected the parity debate that occurred in France during the 2000s. To avoid all essentialism, the French *paritaristes* insisted on the universality of sexual difference – that sexual difference is present in all groups – to prevent singling out women. Those who did not share this view pointed out that many groups were excluded from parliamentary representation, not just women. If all of them were taken into account, the exercise of citizenship would be segmented into "special interests" related not only to gender, but also to class, cultural, ethnic, religious, sexual, and other groupings. As Varikas puts it, this would imprison "individuals in homogeneous, fixed, essential identities." Yet this is precisely the issue: Can one auto-matically assume that female office holders will represent women's view to the exclusion of everything else? Which women, and which points of view, would these be? Do all women share the same views? Indeed, must we not accept that, like men, they have complex and shifting identities? Their class, race, and ethnic backgrounds, as well as their religious persuasion, sexual orienta-tion, handicaps, and a host of other factors will influence them to conceive of politics – and the common good – in differing ways. Similarly, can one state that women's views are necessarily better, more humane, more compassionate, and more egalitarian than those of men? Do the political positions of women in office differ fundamentally from those of men? Would women automatically do politics differently from men? Answering these questions with an unqualified "yes" would be difficult to back up with fact.

POLITICS AND WOMEN

Although no women ran for office in the 1944 provincial election, the political parties, notably the Bloc populaire and the Union nationale, found it worth their while to appeal to the new female electorate. According to reports in Le Devoir on 27 July and the Montreal Gazette on 1 August, the leaders of these two parties, André Laurendeau and Maurice Duplessis, reminded women re-peatedly that the Liberals had tolerated the imposition of con-scription and asked them to contribute to its defeat. In the name of national defence, or even revenge, the two parties tried to at-tract the women's vote – the same justification that had been used in the past to decry their suffrage. A quick glance at the media coverage of subsequent election campaigns reveals that the parties were largely unconcerned with women's suffrage there-after and did not try to attract the female electorate. The Union nationale, which took power in 1944 and held it for the next six-teen years, apparently paid little attention to women. Similarly, its Liberal adversary did not in any obvious way seek their support to defeat the Unionists. Here and there – as in *La Revue Moderne* in June 1948 and *L'Écho des Agriculteurs* in June 1956 – a column urged women to go out and vote, but no more than that.

Surprisingly, the election of Marie-Claire Kirkland-Casgrain in a 1961 by-election did not arouse controversy; the press simply reported the facts without comment. In 1978, the Radio-Canada television program *Femme d'aujourd'hui* interviewed journalist Normand Girard about her appointment as a cabinet minister. In his opinion, it showed that the Liberal Party wanted to give women a voice in the cabinet. But also, "having elected the first woman under its banner, it was only normal that she be integrated [into the cabinet]." On the basis of this, one might assume that her experience and skills as a lawyer had nothing to do with her appointment, but in fact she was among the best qualified to steer Bill 16 through the legislative process. This statute ended the legal incapacity of married women and marked a major turning point in Quebec women's quest for equality. Among Kirkland-Casgrain's main accomplishments was preparing the ground for the 1969 passage of another statute that abolished the legal regime of community of assets, replacing it with partnership of acquests. In 1973, she was responsible for adoption of the law establishing the Conseil du statut de la femme, which was to advise government on issues regarding women's status. She was thus following through on the Bird Commission recommendation that councils on the status of women be created in all provinces.

We must remember that the presence of women in politics was accompanied by a feminist resurgence that demanded equality between the sexes, along with numerous social, economic, and legal measures to attain this objective. As shown by Kirkland-Casgrain's terms in the Legislative Assembly (and later the National Assembly), female members certainly spearheaded advances on a number of issues concerning women or male-female relations. For instance, Lise Bacon, minister of social affairs, crafted the first Quebec policy on daycare centres, called the

Bacon Plan, which was adopted in the early 1970s. For her part, Pauline Marois, as minister of family and children in Lucien Bouchard's Parti québécois (PQ) government, created the Centres de la petite enfance during the late 1990s. The Bacon Plan was widely criticized by feminists and working-class groups, and Marois's innovation was blamed for preserving private daycare centres and for the slow pace at which the government opened new places in public daycares. Nonetheless, these measures made a difference in the lives of many women, as they still do today, and are the envy of other provinces. According to *Femmes et vie politique,* published in 2010 by the National Assembly, at least ten bills that were presented by female ministers and that contained real advances for women were unanimously adopted. Among them were the Loi sur la capacité juridique des femmes mariées (1964), giving married women legal status; the Loi sur l'égalité économique des époux (or Loi du patrimoine familial), giving spouses economic equality (1989); the Loi sur le paiement des pensions alimentaires, enforcing the payment of alimony (1995); a statute on wage parity (1996); and the Loi sur l'assurance parentale, providing for parental leaves (2001).

Despite their imperfections, these statutes had a significant impact on women's lives, and it is certainly reassuring to know that all members of the assembly, both men and women, supported them. According to reports by female members, they have sometimes relied heavily on the support of and even lobbying by feminist groups to get such measures passed. These members also note, with pride, that they have managed to form a common front to get laws adopted. This alliance transcends party lines, which is quite rare in parliamentary systems. Perhaps one of the most brilliant and moving manifestations of female solidarity in the National Assembly occurred in December 2014, on the twenty-fifth anniversary of the massacre of fourteen young women at the École polytechnique de Montréal. On that occasion, each of the thirty-one female members present, all parties combined, stood up to read parts of an essay written by feminist journalist Françoise Guénette denouncing violence against women, an initiative of Françoise David of Québec solidaire.

Women ministers, in collaboration with their sister members, have certainly played a major role in the adoption of a number of laws favourable to women, and a few women have reached the pinnacle of political power. For instance, Monique Gagnon-Tremblay, a Liberal, was appointed minister of finance in 1993 and chair of the Treasury Board in 1994 – two firsts. In addition, Pauline Marois occupied many authoritative positions in Parizeau's PQ government, as did Monique Jérôme-Forget in Charest's Liberal cabinet between 2003 and 2009. Marois was also minister of revenue, as was Rita Dionne-Marsolais (PQ) in 1998 and 1999. Nonetheless, the appointment of women to the highest positions of power does not always go unquestioned. And it must be acknowledged that the vast majority have found themselves heading departments that have a social, socio-economic, or cultural mandate. Fewer have held economic or state portfolios whose decisions profoundly affect social structures and relations between men and women. The habit of confining female members to family-related portfolios thus reproduces the age-old sexual separation of roles and spheres. When Lise Payette wrote a book about her experience in René Lévesque's cabinet between 1976 and 1981, this is why she titled it *Le pouvoir? Connais pas!* (Power? Don't Know It!). It should be noted that though ministers are selected by the leader of government (who, with one exception, has always been male), it is possible that women themselves have sought these less powerful positions because they are socialized to feel at ease in them.

We can justifiably say that the presence of women in the National Assembly and the coalitions they have built have helped produce significant legislative changes with regard to the legal and economic status of Quebec women. Nevertheless, true equality between the sexes and the end of all discrimination against women have certainly not been achieved. The Charte des droits et des libertés de la personne, adopted unanimously in the National Assembly in 1975, accorded the right to equality. It was supposed to protect against discriminatory social practices, and because it took precedence over other laws it guarded against their discriminatory effects. But in reality, a wide gulf often separates the great principles stated in charters from what happens in daily life.

In *Canada's Rights Revolution*, historian Dominique Clément maintains that the Quebec charter of rights and freedoms was adopted in good part thanks to pressure by the Ligue des droits de l'homme du Québec (LDH, now known as the Ligue des droits et libertés), which began to prioritize it during the early 1970s. In Clément's view, the LDH became "the most egalitarian rights association in Canada" because it promoted not only civil and political freedoms, like most groups of its type, but also social, economic, and cultural rights. Thus, it defended collective rights, not just individual ones, and could integrate women's rights into its demands. These included the right to abortion, access to daycare, and, more generally, equality of the sexes, which became a cardinal LDH principle. However, an 11 December 1974 episode of *Femme d'aujourd'hui* showed that the charter bill tabled by the Quebec government, though inspired by an LDH proposal, was far from responding to its expectations or to those of feminists. LDH president Maurice Champagne castigated the bill because, unlike the text submitted by his organization, it did not clearly affirm equality between men and women. In his view, the word "man," used universally for "human being" in the title of the proposed chapter, represented "a narcissistic and misogynous usurpation."

In fact, the Quebec charter was amended several times before its gaps were corrected. Grounds for discrimination were added, affecting, more specifically, women, sexual orientation (in 1977), and age and pregnancy (both in 1982). The charter was the first in Canada to include sexual orientation. In 2008, the National

Assembly unanimously adopted another amendment. Now, a new paragraph in the preamble and a new article clearly affirmed the principle of the equality between men and women. The change meant that this principle took precedence over any other rights protected by the charter. When it was presented, the Bouchard-Taylor Commission had just submitted its report. The commission had been mandated by the Quebec government to study the "accommodations" granted to religious and cultural minorities by public facilities and institutions (such as schools and hospitals) so that they could worship and preserve their customs despite the established rules. The commissioners, historian Gérard Bouchard and philosopher Charles Taylor, had concluded that such accommodations were less widespread and much less restrictive to society than was generally thought, but many citizens continued to contest the very principle of their existence. The wearing of the Islamic veil in public was a particular target of opponents to "reasonable accommodation," who viewed it as a manifestation of oppression of Muslim women. The government of Jean Charest hoped to put an end to the debate with its amendment to the charter, but instead it exacerbated divisions, including among feminists. Thus, although the Conseil du statut de la femme (CSF) it endorsed the modification to the charter, the Fédération des femmes du Québec felt that equality between men and women was a non-negotiable principle, but it also denounced the fact that the political right was using it to help justify its racist position regarding immigrants, particularly Muslims. It also deplored that the formal equality offered by the Quebec charter did not translate into true equality, as systemic discrimination stood in the way, especially for immigrant and racialized women. In November 2013, the Parti québécois government tabled Bill 60, the Quebec Charter of Values, which sought to affirm the principle of secularism. This translated to barring government employees and staff in the health care and education sectors from wearing religious symbols, such as the Islamic veil, "which, by their conspicuous nature, overtly indicate a religious affiliation." The new charter provoked an even more virulent debate. It was never adopted, but it divided the feminist movement more than ever and gave rise to another group, Pour les droits des femmes du Québec. On the one hand, the Fédération des femmes du Québec said that it agreed with the principle of secularism, but it opposed the new charter because it denied women's freedom to choose for themselves whether to wear the veil. On the other hand, Pour les droits des femmes du Québec advocated a form of secularism that rejected all expression of religion in the public space – the only way, it felt, to preserve women's rights and ensure their equality. This dispute, which divided both white and racialized feminists, led to the resignation of Liberal Fatima Houda-Pépin, the only Muslim in the National Assembly, because she felt that her party was going too far by accepting the wearing of religious symbols by government employees who had coercive power. The question still raises lively debate.

The issue of fundamental rights and the general principles that should govern "coexistence" thus provoked much controversy in Quebec during the mid-2000s, and the cracks seemed to be widening in feminist and political circles. Even in the assembly, female members, though sometimes forming a common front, as mentioned above, did not necessarily identify with feminism. Some wished to distance themselves for ideological reasons, whereas others downplayed their allegiance to avoid generating arguments that might harm them or their party. In a 2011 essay, historian Micheline Dumont examined the feminist commitment of Quebec female politicians. She states that of the 104 members for whom she had information, only 24 called themselves feminists or belonged to feminist groups. Five saw themselves as sympathizers. The other 75 gave no clue that they supported this ideology and movement. Further, Dumont observes that of the nine women who had held the status of women portfolio since the late 1970s, only three "gave evidence of their feminist commitment." From 2011 until the October 2018 election of the government of the Coalition avenir Québec, four female ministers have held this portfolio. Of them, only Agnès Maltais (PQ) and Hélène David (Liberal), appointed in fall 2017, can be categorized as openly feminist. One of the other two, Lise Thériault, has stated clearly that she is not a feminist. "I am much more egalitarian than feminist," she declared in February 2016, as reported by Canadian Press, shortly after the government slashed the CSF budget.

Thériault later reconsidered this statement, but her position confirms what many researchers have noticed: female members often refuse to identify as feminist because, they say, their job is to represent all their constituents – both male and female – and especially to avoid giving the impression that they prioritize women. Dumont points to the pride expressed by Liberal premier Jean Charest when he appointed a perfectly gender-equal cabinet in 2007 and 2010 (the cabinet of the 2018 Coalition avenir Québec government also included an equal number of men and women ministers). She hypothesizes that displaying feminist convictions or taking feminist actions can be positively received – but only when men do it. Women frequently encounter a far less positive response, hence their tendency to camouflage their positions. "This would appear to be," Dumont concludes, "one of the last avatars of the 'double standard' between men and women."

Although relatively few female members openly embrace feminism, women's entrance into politics coincided with the 1960s renaissance of the feminist movement, which certainly helped to open the doors to power – a fact that would be hard for them to ignore. Even if they refuse to identify with the movement, they cannot escape the influence of feminist analysis and its denunciations of gender inequalities. These feed social debates and force the adoption of laws that, though not always optimal, aim to correct the most flagrant discrimination.

In addition, women's progress in politics occurred during the late 1960s, when a new Quebec nationalism, embodied mainly in the PQ, was asserting itself. The Indigenous movement was also beginning to demand respect for the ancestral rights of the First Nations, which were affirming their own nationalism. White feminists who supported or were active in the PQ were attracted by its desire to modernize Quebec, including relations between men and women, and by its emphasis on equality and independence, which feminists also demanded for women. Nevertheless, aligning their feminist and nationalist positions often posed a challenge, as the latter were too commonly based on a restrictive concept of gender roles that was difficult to reconcile with the emancipation of women. While subscribing to the modernization of Quebec society, which entailed the establishment of a welfare state likely to support equality between the sexes, a nationalist fringe continued to fear the total freedom of women, as it would interfere with their primary vocation – the reproduction of the nation. As we have seen, Indigenous women were running into similar problems. Although they generally supported the demands of the male nationalist leaders, they often criticized their lack of sensitivity to women's particular situation and their mistrust of, or even hostility toward, women who had married outside the community. It should be added that nationalism was a divisive factor among feminists themselves. Like many First Nations women, some felt excluded from or indifferent to this project. Immigrant women have also expressed reservations. In 1990, for example, Lise Payette was appointed honorary president of the festivities to celebrate the fiftieth anniversary of women's suffrage. Under the banner of the Collectif des femmes immigrantes, groups of immigrant women withdrew in protest and expressed anger at the choice of Payette. They objected to her because she had co-authored the screenplay for a documentary that prophesied the disappearance of francophone Quebecers unless they had more children and accepted only those immigrants who could integrate with francophone society. Rifts also appeared during both sovereignty referendums in Quebec, held in 1980 and 1995. During public consultations in 1980, Payette likened women who opposed sovereignty to "Yvettes." A fictional character who appeared in some textbooks, Yvette was a docile girl who delighted in domestic tasks. This unflattering comparison incited women in the Liberal Party to organize various activist assemblies during which they loudly and cheerfully appropriated the name "Yvette" to better support the "no" camp, contributing largely to its victory. In an article written for the magazine *L'Action nationale,* Micheline Dumont stated that the Yvettes thus enabled women to enter "the political memory of history." Fifteen years later, during the second referendum, women of various minority groups shared their fears about a nationalism that sometimes verged on xenophobia, and Indigenous women refused to become involved in a debate that, they felt, did not really concern them. In short, these disputes certainly proved that women were far from forming a homogeneous group with a single point of view – which their entrance into politics and membership in parties with differing philosophies and ideologies had already shown.

⌘

Although decades have passed since Quebec women obtained the right to vote, the story is still ongoing. Women still experience difficulty in carving out a place for themselves in political parties, in getting elected, and in being appointed as ministers, especially for portfolios with an economic vocation. In addition, numerous groups of racialized, immigrant, Indigenous, and disadvantaged women always find it difficult to make their voices heard. The low representation of women in Parliament has driven many feminists to demand parity, an option that is not supported by everyone. For today, as yesterday, women are not unanimous. Just as many once opposed the very idea of voting because they did not see the purpose of it, some refuse to support more egalitarian representation through a statute or measures that would impose it. In their view, parity would devalue the participation of women in political bodies by giving the impression that they owe their positions to a form of accommodation.

Nevertheless, women's presence in politics, even as a minority, has coincided with the adoption of measures favourable to them. Although it is difficult to establish a direct link between these two phenomena, one may presume that without female representatives, these laws would not have been adopted or would have been delayed. Some would have been formulated differently, perhaps with less impact or a more negative effect on the female population. Despite their disagreements on many questions, including that of Quebec as a nation, female representatives do seem to have achieved a minimal solidarity that has somewhat attenuated their divergences of views, if only temporarily, to the benefit of all women. Although the difference between the sexes has not equalized the conditions or standardized the opinions of women, the inequalities to which they have long been subject seem at least to have made them highly aware of some common denominators that set them apart from men.

THE STRUGGLE FOR WOMEN'S suffrage lasted longer and was more difficult in Quebec than in the Protestant regions of the Western world, but it followed the same time frame as that in European Catholic countries as a whole – though for different reasons. In France, Belgium, and Italy, women were not enfranchised until the 1940s, due to fears that they would favour right-wing parties allied with the Catholic Church, though even the church itself accepted their suffrage. In Quebec, the absence of a well-structured left embodied in a major political party meant that support for the suffragists was splintered, as most politicians and members of the upper Catholic hierarchy had no interest in giving them access to the polls. On the contrary: whereas parliaments in English Canada had acceded to the demands of suffragists, the political and religious authorities in Quebec erected a wall against the women's vote. This constituted another means of affirming the difference – even the superiority – of the French Canadian people. Uncertain of their capacity to impose their views on Ottawa, francophone politicians sought to rule supreme at home, in the only province where their ethnic group was a majority. There, they would work to preserve the values and institutions in which their authority was rooted. In fact, the suffragist demand that women be permitted to share power threatened their self-image as sole protectors of the nation, challenging a fundamental aspect of their masculinity. The Catholic Church, which counted on women to reproduce both life and cultural and religious values, found it difficult to believe that they were capable of devoting themselves to something other than the home.

For the early French Canadian suffragists, such as Marie Lacoste Gérin-Lajoie, enfranchisement would empower women in their fields of jurisdiction, both in the heart of the private sphere and in the public space. Then, with Thérèse Casgrain and Idola Saint-Jean, the vote was seen more as an indispensable tool for having all their rights respected and for controlling their fate. Although the ultimate goal of the battle – access to the ballot box – remained the same, the reasons for supporting it changed over time. In the early 1920s, the main argument was that having the vote would allow women to better accomplish their maternal duties. By the end of the decade, advocacy had turned to all aspects of women's rights. From this point of view, even if the actions and strategies of the second-generation suffragists remained very measured, it can be said that the struggle was somewhat radicalized. Indeed, rather than reinforcing the male authorities' vision of the world, the suffragists sought to impose a representation of women's role in society that rejected the very foundations of that vision.

The female opponents of suffrage were generally not happy to see their conception of themselves and their place in society disrupted. Those who lived in rural areas, in particular, saw enfranchisement not as a right but as a negation of their femininity. In their opinion, voting belonged to the world of men – a world of corruption, booze, and violence. They wanted nothing to do with it. The church, as well as members of the Legislative Assembly, helped to propagate this highly unattractive image to keep women away, but it also corresponded to such a widespread reality that many women saw becoming involved in politics as inappropriate for them. The few reactions by these opponents that have survived testify not so much to submission to the clergy or to men in general, but to a conviction that women had nothing concrete to gain from suffrage, whereas they had much to lose. Behind this attitude thus seems to have been a mistrust of the democratic system itself. They felt that having the vote had nothing to do with making themselves heard by elected representatives.

In any case, Indigenous women's indifference to the vote sprang from their certainty that nothing good would come from the white colonialist government. Not only did the reserve system keep their communities in a state of dependence, but it also helped to destructure gender relations to their detriment. Also, the Quebec government tended to neglect Indigenous women's role in their communities and negotiated only with male chiefs, when it negotiated at all. Like their male counterparts, Indigenous women therefore did not demand the right to elect representatives, in whom they had no confidence and who did not know how to speak for them. Instead, they united in the 1970s to demand that Ottawa amend the Indian Act so that it would recognize their status as equal to men's. At the same time, they sought to find a place on band councils, both to ensure that the changes achieved would be implemented and to raise other problems that they were experiencing on the reserves.

Have women changed politics? Or has politics changed women? Perhaps it is too early for a definitive answer. Enfranchisement did not immediately translate into seats in parliaments and cabinets, as many years elapsed before a woman was elected to the Legislative Assembly. Almost sixty years after this "first," women who want to enter politics still face numerous obstacles, especially if they are minority – racialized or other – the proof being that they achieved parity only recently. The battle for suffrage is over, but the next battle – representation that takes account of women's diversity – has yet to be won.

Although feminists opened the path for women politicians, not all women politicians are feminists. Should they be? To answer "yes" would say little about women's freedom of thought and the plurality of their opinions. No similar unanimity has ever been required of men. Nonetheless, it is a bit ironic that some elected female politicians say they do not recognize themselves in the battles that ultimately enabled them to occupy positions of power. Furthermore, whether or not they call themselves feminists, women politicians can put aside their differences and partisan allegiances to form a united front when they feel that the interests of women as a whole are at stake. Thus, we can say that they sometimes perform politics differently, and also that they have made a real difference. In other words, though they certainly have not completely changed how politics is done, politics has perhaps not completely changed them either.

ACKNOWLEDGMENTS

I OWE THE EXISTENCE of this book to Veronica Strong-Boag, a pioneer in women's history and professor emeritus at the University of British Columbia. It was her idea to bring together a team of historians to produce a series of books on the history of women's suffrage in Canada – an idea for which I would like to thank her. I would like to acknowledge the Faculté des Arts et des Sciences of the Université de Montréal for awarding me a research grant, which enabled me to enhance the content of this book. I also acknowledge the Canadian Federation for the Humanities and Social Sciences for a grant through the Awards to Scholarly Publications Program, using funds provided by the Social Sciences and Humanities Research Council of Canada. I am indebted to Nathalie Picard, who graciously agreed to take a look at her research files to help me learn a little more about Indigenous women who voted in 1824. Finally, a big thank you to Marilou Tanguay, who was my research assistant for this project and who proved to be an outstanding and enthusiastic contributor.

SOURCES AND
FURTHER READING

THIS BOOK IS BASED on studies regarding the issue of suffrage in Quebec and Canada, as well as in other countries, such as France and Ireland. In addition, the author conducted complementary research in the archives of suffragist associations and on parliamentary debates that have been reconstructed since the first researchers became interested in the question. The digitization of a number of periodicals (magazines, Montreal and regional weeklies and dailies), now available on the website of the Bibliothèque et Archives nationales du Québec (BAnQ), also expanded the research corpus. In some cases, keyword searches flushed out little explored opinions or phenomena, enriching the narrative.

PRIMARY SOURCES

Writing this book required the examination of many newspapers, periodicals, and magazines. Material held in various archives and online was also helpful.

For the first half of the nineteenth century, the partisan press, including *La Minerve, Le Canadien,* the *Quebec Mercury,* and the *Vindicator,* was particularly useful. For the period after 1880, the author consulted the dailies *La Patrie, La Presse, Le Canada, Le Devoir, Le Soleil,* the *Montreal Gazette,* the *Montreal Herald,* and the *Montreal Star,* and the weeklies *Le Bulletin des agriculteurs* and *L'Écho de Saint-Maurice.* Key information came from the periodicals of feminist associations *(La bonne parole, La Gazette des femmes, La Sphère féminine)* and of labour organizations *(Le Monde ouvrier).* Finally, several women's magazines were scrutinized, including *Le coin du feu, Le Journal de Françoise, Mon Magazine,* and *La Revue Moderne.* The archival collections of various Montreal associations that fought for suffrage – the Montreal Suffrage Association, the Canadian Alliance for Women's Vote in Quebec, and the League for Women's Rights – contain documents that supplied much information and many quotations. For the Montreal Suffrage Association, see Archives de Montréal, "Fonds BM101–Fonds Montreal Suffrage Association, 1913–1919," https://archivesdemontreal.ica -atom.org/fonds-de-la-montreal-suffrage-association-1913 -1919. For the Canadian Alliance, consult Archives de Montréal, "Fonds BM102–Fonds Idola Saint-Jean, [190-]–1958," https:// archivesdemontreal.ica-atom.org/fonds-idola-saint-jean-190 -1958. And for the league, visit Archives de Montréal, "Fonds BM014–Fonds Ligue des droits de la femme, 1922– [196-]," https:// archivesdemontreal.ica-atom.org/fonds-de-la-ligue-des-droits -de-la-femme-1922-196.

The poll books for the 1824 election in Huntingdon were at the head office of the BAnQ, where they were in the process of being restored. The archives of historian Catherine Cleverdon, who was the first to research women's suffrage in Canada, are at Library and Archives Canada (LAC, MG30, D160).

Among the most useful printed government documents were *Statuts du Bas-Canada* (4 Gul. IV, 1834, c. 28, and 12 Vict., 1849, c. 27); the *Report of the Royal Commission on the Status of Women in Canada* (Ottawa: Information Canada, 1970); and, with regard to Quebec, the *Débats reconstitués de l'Assemblée législative,* specifically on enfranchisement, female workers, the Civil Code, and women's access to the bar (1929–39).

The *Act to Amend the Charter of Human Rights and Freedoms* (Bill 63, 2008, c. 15) also provided elements that were essential to the analysis, as did Muriel Garon and Pierre Bosset, "Étude no 2: Le droit à l'égalité: des progrès remarquables, des inégalités persistantes," in Commission des droits de la personne et des droits de la jeunesse du Québec, *Après 25 ans: La charte québécoise des droits et libertés* (Quebec City: The Commission, 2003), 2:65–70. I read numerous online government documents, including *Chronique Montréalité no 30: Les femmes et la politique municipale*, at http://archivesdemontreal.com/2015/03/09/chronique -montrealite-no-30-les-femmes-et-la-politique-municipale/; and *La démocratie à Montréal de 1830 à nos jours, Les femmes sur la scène politique locale*, at http://www2.ville.montreal.qc.ca/archives/ democratie/democratie_fr/expo/crises-reformes/femmes/index. shtm. The "History" section of the Assemblée nationale du Québec website was used intensively, at http://www.assnat.qc.ca/fr/ patrimoine/index.html. The same is true for the site of the Directeur général des élections du Québec, at http://www4.gouv. qc.ca/fr/Portail/citoyens/programme-service/Pages/Info. aspx?sqctype=mo&sqcid=116; and for Assemblée nationale du Québec, "Femmes et vie politique: De la conquête du droit de vote à nos jours, 1940–2010," http://www.paricilademocratie.com/ document/321.

The last chapter of the book was greatly enhanced by information in various documents from the Conseil du statut de la femme, including *Droit à l'égalité entre les hommes et les femmes et liberté religieuse* (Quebec City: Conseil du statut de la femme, 2007), https://www.csf.gouv.qc.ca/wp-content/uploads/avis -droit-a-legalite-entre-les-femmes-et-les-hommes-et-liberte -religieuse.pdf; Working Group of Elected Women of the Assembly of First Nations of Québec and Labrador and the Conseil du statut de la femme, *Encountering Each Other: Discussions with Elected Aboriginal Women in Québec* (Quebec City: Conseil du statut de la femme, 2010), https://www.csf.gouv.qc.ca/wp-content/uploads/ etudes-encountering-each-other-discussions-with-elected -aboriginal-women-in-quebec.pdf; and *La sous-représentation des femmes dans les municipalités aux conseils municipaux et dans les mairies* (Quebec City: Conseil du statut de la femme, 2012), https://www.csf.gouv.qc.ca/wp-content/uploads/la-sous-representation-des-femmes-dans-les-municipalites-aux-conseils-municipaux-et-dans-les-mairies.pdf.

From the Canadian government, *A History of the Vote in Canada*, 2nd ed. (Ottawa: Elections Canada, 2007), available on the Elections Canada website at http://www.elections.ca/content.aspx?section=res&dir=his&document=index&lang=e, is essential for understanding the evolution of Indigenous peoples' right to vote. On the question of Indigenous women, I also consulted the *Gender Equity in Indian Registration Act*, S.C. 2010, c. 18, at http://laws-lois.justice.gc.ca/eng/annualstatutes/2010_18/page-1.html; and Truth and Reconciliation Commission of Canada, *Honouring the Truth, Reconciling for the Future: Summary of the Final Report of the Truth and Reconciliation Commission of Canada* (Toronto: James Lorimer, 2015), at http://www.trc.ca/websites/trcinstitution/File/2015/Honouring_the_Truth_Reconciling_for_the_Future_July_23_2015.pdf.

The brief presented by the Fédération des femmes du Québec to the Bouchard-Taylor Commission in Montreal on 19 October 2007 is at Fédération des femmes du Québec, "Mémoire de la FFQ à la Commission Bouchard-Taylor," http://www.ffq.qc.ca/2007/10/commission-bouchard-taylor/.

Pour les droits des femmes du Québec produced two documents that were examined for this book. Both are online: "Mémoire projet de loi no 60: Charte affirmant les valeurs de laïcité et de neutralité religieuse de l'État ainsi que d'égalité entre les femmes et les hommes et encadrant les demandes d'accommodement," January 2014, http://www.pdfquebec.org/documents/Memoire_PDF_Quebec_Oeuvre.pdf; and "Pour une politique d'immigration qui renforce l'égalité entre les femmes et les hommes," January 2015, http://www.pdfquebec.org/documents/Memoire_2015-01-29.pdf.

The online *Dictionary of Canadian Biography*, at http://www. biographi.ca/en/index.php, was particularly useful for the discussion of Hortense Globensky, Joséphine Marchand-Dandurand, Marie Lacoste Gérin-Lajoie, and Joseph-Alphonse Rodier. The biographies of Carrie Matilda Derick, Florence Fernet-Martel, Irène Joly, and Elizabeth Monk were inspired by Maryse Darsigny, Francine Descarries, Lyne Kurtzman, and Évelyne Tardy, eds., *Ces femmes qui ont bâti Montréal* (Montreal: Éditions du remue-ménage, 1994). The website of the Assemblée nationale du Québec, at http://www.assnat.qc.ca/fr/membres/notices/index. html, provided most of the information for the biographies of Marie-Claire Kirkland-Casgrain, Françoise David, and Pauline Marois. For Kirkland-Casgrain and David, complementary information came from the online *Canadian Encyclopedia,* https://www. thecanadianencyclopedia.ca/en. This source was used for the biography of Idola Saint-Jean, which was also based on Gilles Gallichan, "Idola Saint-Jean: Femme de cœur et femme de tête," *Bulletin de la Bibliothèque de l'Assemblée nationale du Québec* 39, 1 (2010): 16–23; Michèle Jean, "Idola Saint-Jean, féministe (1880–1945)," in *Mon héroïne: les lundis de l'histoire des femmes an 1, Conférences du Théâtre expérimental des femmes* (Montreal: Éditions du remue-ménage, 1981), 117–47; Marie Lavigne and Michèle Stanton-Jean, *Idola Saint-Jean, L'insoumise* (Montreal: Boréal, 2017); and Diane Lamoureux, "Idola Saint-Jean et le radicalisme féministe de l'entre-deux-guerres," *Recherches féministes* 4, 2 (1991): 45–60. The biographies of Ellen Gabriel and Lady Ishbel Aberdeen were inspired by the website Women Suffrage and Beyond: Confronting the Democratic Deficit, http://womensuffrage. org/?s=democratic+deficit&SearchSubmit=searc; and by Julie Bruneau-Papineau's page at BAnQ, "Famille de Louis-Joseph Papineau," http://www.banq.qc.ca/histoire_quebec/parcours_ thematiques/Papineau/bruneau_julie.jsp. For Grace Julia Parker Drummond, see McCord Museum, "Fonds de la famille Drummond (P015)," http://collections.musee-mccord.qc.ca/scripts/explore.

php?Lang=2&tableid=18&elementid=154__true. The obituary for Grace Ritchie-England supplied the main elements for her biography: see Maysie S. MacSporran, "'Vale, Amica Carissima': Dr Grace Ritchie England's 80 Years of Life Filled with Absorbing Interests," *McGill News,* Spring 1948. Many sources were used for the biography of Thérèse Casgrain, including Fondation Thérèse Casgrain, "Biographie: Dates importantes dans la vie de Thérèse F. Casgrain," http://www.fondationtheresecasgrain.org/bio.html; and Library and Archives Canada, "Celebrating Women's Achievements: Marie Thérèse (Forget) Casgrain," http://www.collections canada.gc.ca/women/030001-1301-e.html. Nicole Forget, *Thérèse Casgrain: La gauchiste en collier de perles* (Montreal: Fides, 2013), gives a much more complete overview. For a biography of Jeanne Sauvé, see Library and Archives Canada, "Celebrating Women's Achievements: The Rt. Hon. Jeanne Sauvé," https://www.collections canada.gc.ca/femmes/030001-1313-e.html. The biography of Mary Two-Axe Earley is based on Merna Forster, *100 More Canadian Heroines: Famous and Forgotten Faces* (Toronto: Dundurn Press, 2011), 133–35.

Other sources must also be mentioned, such as Radio-Canada, "Enchâssée dans la Charte," 10 June 2008, http://ici.radio-canada. ca/nouvelles/Politique/2008/06/10/001-egalite-sexes-quebec. shtml; and transcriptions for the 18 April 1974, 11 December 1974, and 21 March 1978 broadcasts of *Femme d'aujourd'hui.*

Finally, the Universal Declaration of Human Rights, quoted in the introduction, is at United Nations, "Universal Declaration of Human Rights," http://www.un.org/en/universal-declaration -human-rights/.

GENERAL WORKS

For a synthesis of the history of women's suffrage worldwide, see Jad Adams, *Women and the Vote: A World History* (Oxford: Oxford University Press, 2014). Catherine Cleverdon is the only historian to have written a pan-Canadian synthesis of women's suffrage:

The Woman Suffrage Movement in Canada (Toronto: University of Toronto Press, 1974 [1950]). Books on women's history also address this question. For Canada, see Gail Cuthbert Brandt, Naomi Black, Paula Bourne, and Magda Fahrni, *Canadian Women: A History* (Toronto: Nelson Education, 2011). For Quebec, see Denyse Baillargeon, *A Brief History of Women in Quebec* (Waterloo: Wilfrid Laurier University Press, 2014). Micheline Dumont wrote a history of the Quebec women's movement that deals with the struggle for the franchise: *Le féminisme québécois raconté à Camille* (Montreal: Éditions du remue-ménage, 2008). The short book by Alain Beaulieu, *Les Autochtones du Québec* (Quebec City/Montreal: Musée de la Civilisation/Fides, 1997), provides a good introduction to the history of Indigenous peoples of Quebec.

INTRODUCTION

The works cited in this section are not referred to in later chapters. Among these is Susan Mann Trofimenkoff, *The Dream of Nation: A Social and Intellectual History of Quebec* (Montreal and Kingston: McGill-Queen's University Press, 2002). Its historical synthesis of the national question includes the issue of gender. For the ideology of separate spheres in the nineteenth century, see Linda K. Kerber, "Separate Spheres, Female Worlds, Woman's Place: The Rhetoric of Women's History," *Journal of American History* 75, 1 (1988): 9–39. Seth Koven and Sonya Michel look at the links between maternalism and women's social and political action in several countries in "Womanly Duties: Maternalist Politics and the Origin of Welfare States in France, Germany, Great Britain, and the United States, 1880–1920," *American Historical Review* 95, 4 (1990): 1076–114. On maternalism, see also Molly Ladd-Taylor, *Mother-Work: Women, Child Welfare, and the State, 1890–1930* (Chicago: University of Illinois Press, 1994); Linda Kealey, ed., *A Not Unreasonable Claim: Women and Reform in Canada* (Toronto: Women's Press, 1979); and Louise Toupin, "Mères ou citoyennes? Une critique du discours historique nord-américain (1960–1990) sur le mouvement féministe (1850–1960)" (PhD diss., Université du Québec à Montréal, 1994). Finally, with regard to women's citizenship, see Kathleen Canning and Sonya O. Rose, "Gender, Citizenship and Subjectivity: Some Historical and Theoretical Considerations," *Gender and History* 13, 3 (2003): 427–43; Linda K. Kerber, "The Meanings of Citizenship," *Journal of American History* 84, 3 (1997): 833–54; and Anne-Marie Kinahan, "Transcendent Citizenship: Suffrage, the National Council of Women of Canada, and the Politics of Organized Womanhood," *Journal of Canadian Studies/Revue d'études canadiennes* 42, 3 (2008): 5–27.

On the conservatism of activist suffragists in English Canada, see Carol Lee Bacchi, *Liberation Deferred? The Ideas of the English-Canadian Suffragists, 1877–1918* (Toronto: University of Toronto Press, 1983); and the critique of this work by Ernest Forbes, "The Ideas of Carol Bacchi and the Suffragists of Halifax: A Review Essay on *Liberation Deferred? The Ideas of the English-Canadian Suffragists, 1877–1918*," *Atlantis* 10, 2 (1985): 119–26. With regard to the racism of these feminists, see Mariana Valverde, "'When the Mother of the Race Is Free': Race, Reproduction, and Sexuality in First-Wave Feminism," in *Gender Conflicts: New Essays in Women's History*, ed. Franca Iacovetta and Mariana Valverde (Toronto: University of Toronto Press, 1992), 3–26; and Cecily Devereux, "New Women, New World: Maternal Feminism and the New Imperialism in the White Settler Colonies," *Women's Studies International Forum* 22, 2 (1999): 174–84. For a more detailed analysis of this subject, see Janice Fiamengo, "Rediscovering Our Foremothers Again: Racial Ideas of Canada's Early Feminists, 1885–1945," in *Rethinking Canada: The Promise of Women's History*, 5th ed., ed. Mona Gleason and Adele Perry (Don Mills: Oxford University Press, 2006), 144–62.

Finally, Sirma Bilge's article "Théorisations féministes de l'intersectionnalité," *Diogène* 225, 1 (2009): 70–88, offers an excellent introduction to the concept of intersectionality.

ONE: PIONEERS OF SUFFRAGE

To learn more about how colonization changed the status of Indigenous women, see Roland Viau, *Femmes de personne: Sexes, genres et pouvoirs en Iroquoisie ancienne* (Montreal: Boréal, 2000).

On the nineteenth-century electoral system in the British North American colonies, see Colin Grittner, "Privilege at the Polls: Culture, Citizenship, and the Electoral Franchise in Mid-Nineteenth-Century British North America" (PhD diss., McGill University, 2015). For an in-depth analysis of the women's vote in the first half of the nineteenth century, see Nathalie Picard, "Les femmes et le vote au Bas-Canada de 1792 à 1849" (master's thesis, Université de Montréal, 1992). In "Pour une nouvelle synthèse sur les processus électoraux du XIXe siècle québécois," *Journal of the Canadian Historical Association* 16, 1 (2005): 75–100, Renaud Séguin examines the application of electoral law as a whole in Lower Canada during the same period.

For a good understanding of the steps that led to the abolition of the female franchise following the 1832 election, consult Bettina Bradbury, "Women at the Hustings: Gender, Citizenship, and the Montreal By-elections of 1832," in *Rethinking Canada: The Promise of Women's History*, 4th ed., ed. Mona Gleason and Adele Perry (Don Mills: Oxford University Press, 2006), 73–94. Bradbury also offers the best dissection of the loss of dower rights, in "Debating Dower: Patriarchy, Capitalism and Widows' Rights in Lower Canada," in *Power, Place and Identity:*

Historical Studies of Social and Legal Regulation in Quebec, ed. Tamara Myers, Kate Boyer, Mary Anne Poutanen, and Steven Watt (Montreal: Montreal History Group, 1998), 55–78. Bradbury revisits these two subjects in her more recent book, *Wife to Widow: Lives, Laws and Politics in Nineteenth-Century Montreal* (Vancouver: UBC Press, 2011).

Allan Greer analyzes the Patriote leaders' conception of women's place in society, in "La république des hommes: Les Patriotes de 1837 face aux femmes," *Revue d'histoire de l'Amérique française* 44, 4 (Spring 1997): 507–28. On women and the rebellions, see also Francis Back, "L'étoffe de la liberté; politique textile et comportements vestimentaires du mouvement patriote," *Bulletin d'histoire politique* 10, 2 (Winter 2002): 58–71; Mylène Bédard, *Écrire en temps d'insurrections: Pratiques épistolaires et usages de la presse chez les femmes patriotes (1830–1840)* (Montreal: Presses de l'Université de Montréal, 2016); Marilyn Randall, *Les Femmes dans l'espace rebelle: Histoire et Fiction autour des Rébellions de 1837 et 1838* (Montreal: Nota bene, 2013); and Marilyn Randall, "Pantalon, parole et pistolet: l'invention de la femme dans les journaux canadiens à l'époque de la Rébellion de 1837–38," in *Archive et poétique de l'invention,* ed. Marc-André Bernier (Montreal: Nota bene, 2003), 159–82.

On the Institut canadien, see Yvan Lamonde, *Histoire sociale des idées au Québec, 1760–1896,* vol. 1 (Montreal: Fides, 2000). For a good analysis of gendered discourses in Upper Canada during the nineteenth century, see Cecilia Morgan, *Public Men and Virtuous Women: The Gendered Languages of Religion and Politics in Upper Canada, 1791–1850* (Toronto: University of Toronto Press, 1998). Historian Lisa Tetrault relates how the legend of the American feminist meeting in Seneca Falls was built, in *The Myth of Seneca Falls: Memory and the Women's Suffrage Movement, 1848–1898* (Chapel Hill: University of North Carolina Press, 2014). Finally, the dilemma of mother as citizen was raised, no doubt for the first time, by Mary Wollstonecraft in *A Vindication of the Rights of Woman* (Boston: Peter Edes, 1792).

TWO: GIVING WOMEN A VOICE

For charitable works by women at the turn of the twentieth century, see Micheline Dallaire, *Les communautés religieuses et l'assistance sociale à Montréal, 1659–1900* (Montreal: Éditions du Méridien, 1997); Janice Harvey, "Les Églises protestantes et l'assistance aux pauvres à Montréal au xixe siècle," *Études d'histoire religieuse* 69 (2003): 51–67; and Huguette Lapointe-Roy, *Charité bien ordonnée: le premier réseau de lutte contre la pauvreté à Montréal au 19e siècle* (Montreal: Boréal, 1987).

For social action and the philanthropic and reformist engagement of bourgeois women, see Elizabeth Kirkland, "Mothering Citizens: Elite Women in Montreal, 1890–1914" (PhD diss., McGill University, 2011); Yolande Pinard, "Les débuts du mouvement des femmes à Montréal, 1893–1902," in *Travailleuses et féministes: Les femmes dans la société québécoise,* ed. Marie Lavigne and Yolande Pinard (Montreal:

Boréal express, 1983), 177–98. These studies, along with Marie Lavigne, Yolande Pinard, and Jennifer Stoddart, "La Fédération nationale Saint-Jean-Baptiste et les revendications féministes au début du 20e siècle," in Lavigne and Pinard, *Travailleuses et féministes*, 199–216, are also very useful for understanding the beginning of the women's movement in Montreal and the organizations that were created. For the early years of the International Council of Women, see Catherine Jacques, "Construire un réseau international: l'exemple du Conseil international des Femmes (CIF)," in *Le siècle des féminismes*, ed. Éliane Gubin, Catherine Jacques, Florence Rochefort, Brigitte Studer, Françoise Thébaud, and Michelle Zancarini-Fournel (Paris: Éditions de l'Atelier, 2004), 127–41.

Karine Hébert, "Une organisation maternaliste au Québec, la Fédération nationale Saint-Jean-Baptiste (1900–1940)" (master's thesis, Université de Montréal, 1997); and Karine Hébert, "Une organisation maternaliste au Québec: la Fédération nationale Saint-Jean-Baptiste et la bataille pour le vote des femmes," *Revue d'histoire de l'Amérique française* 52, 3 (1999): 315–44, revisit the history of the FNSJB in a maternalist perspective. For an interesting treatment of the life of Marie Lacoste Gérin-Lajoie, who led the FNSJB for almost thirty years, see Anne-Marie Sicotte's novelized biography *Marie Gérin-Lajoie, Conquérante de Liberté* (Montreal: Éditions du remue-ménage, 2005).

On municipal politics, consult Paul-André Linteau, *Histoire de Montréal depuis la Confédération* (Montreal: Boréal, 1992). On the women's vote during the Trois-Rivières referendum against daylight saving time, see Jarrett Rudy, "Maternalisme, conflit de classes et les débuts de l'heure avancée à Trois-Rivières, de 1918 à 1937," *Revue d'histoire de l'Amérique française* 66, 3–4 (2013): 395–417. Tamara Myers examines the role that women played in the passage of Canadian and Quebec laws on juvenile delinquents, in *Caught: Montreal's Modern Girls and the Law, 1869–1945* (Toronto: University of Toronto Press, 2006). Pierre Chemartin and Louis Pelletier discuss the anti-suffrage opposition of anglophone Montrealers, notably women, in "Clubs, Axes, and Umbrellas: The Woman Suffrage Movement as Seen by Montreal Cartoonists (1910–1914)," in *Sketches from an Unquiet Country: Canadian Graphic Satire, 1840–1940*, ed. Dominic Hardy, Annie Gérin, and Lora Senechal Carney (Montreal and Kingston: McGill-Queen's University Press, 2018), 136–69. Finally, on the "family" conception of the vote in nineteenth-century France, see Anne Verjus, *Le cens de la famille: Les femmes et le vote, 1789–1848* (Paris: Belin, 2002).

THREE: BROADENING THE STRUGGLE

On the role played by Mary Ann Shadd Cary in the struggle for the vote in Canada, see Joan Sangster, *One Hundred Years of Struggle: The History of Women and the Vote in Canada* (Vancouver: UBC Press, 2018). On the campaign for the vote in France, see Christine Bard, *Les filles de Marianne: Histoire des féminismes, 1914–1940* (Paris: Fayard, 1995); and Laurence Klejman and Florence Rochefort, *L'égalité en marche, le féminisme sous la Troisième République* (Paris: Presses de la Fondation nationale de Sciences Politiques/Éditions des femmes–Antoinette Fouque, 1989). With regard to the situation in Ireland, see Louise Ryan, "Traditions and Double Moral Standards: The Irish Suffragists' Critique of Nationalism," *Women's History Review* 4, 4 (1995): 487–503.

Tarah Brookfield analyzes the 1917 conflict within the Montreal Local Council of Women regarding the women's vote, in "Divided by the Ballot Box: The Montreal Council of Women and the 1917 Election," *Canadian Historical Review* 89, 4 (2008): 473–501. For a detailed study of the life and thought of journalist Éva Circé-Côté, specifically in connection with suffrage, see Andrée Lévesque, *Éva Circé-Côté: Libre penseuse, 1871–1949* (Montreal: Éditions du remue-ménage, 2010). On Henri Bourassa's position concerning enfranchisement, see Susan Mann Trofimenkoff, "Henri Bourassa et la Question des Femmes," in *Travailleuses et féministes: Les femmes dans la société québécoise*, ed. Marie Lavigne and Yolande Pinard (Montreal: Boréal, 1983), 293–306. For a better understanding of Monsignor Louis-Adolphe Paquet's view, see his "Le féminisme," in Louis-Adolphe Paquet, *Études et appréciations: Nouveaux mélanges canadiens* (Quebec City: Imprimerie franciscaine missionnaire, 1919), 3–43.

On the various steps and events surrounding the struggle for the women's vote during the early 1920s, see Maryse Darsigny, "Du comité provincial du suffrage féminin à la Ligue des droits de la femme, 1922–1940: le second souffle du mouvement féministe au Québec de la première moitié du xxe siècle" (master's thesis, Université du Québec à Montréal, 1995); Luigi Trifiro, "La crise de 1922 dans la lutte pour le suffrage féminin au Québec" (master's thesis, Université de Sherbrooke, 1976); Luigi Trifiro, "Une intervention à Rome dans la lutte pour le suffrage féminin au Québec (1922)," *Revue d'histoire de l'Amérique française* 32, 1 (1978): 3–18; and the works by Karine Hébert cited in the section for Chapter 2. With regard to Jewish feminist and women's associations in Montreal, see Sarah Filotas, "Les organisations féminines de la communauté juive montréalaise, 1918–1948" (master's thesis, Université de Montréal, 1998).

On the opposition of the Cercles de fermières to women's suffrage, see Ghislaine Desjardins, "Les Cercles de fermières et l'action féminine en milieu rural, 1915–1944," in *Travailleuses et féministes: Les femmes dans la société québécoise*, ed. Marie Lavigne and Yolande Pinard (Montreal: Boréal, 1983), 217–44. Yolande Cohen and Chantal Maillé examine the FNSJB creation of civics courses, in "Les cours d'instruction civique de la Fédération nationale Saint-Jean-Baptiste: Une voie d'accès à la citoyenneté politique pour les femmes du Québec," *Recherches Féministes* 12, 2 (1999): 39–59. Finally, Gilles Gallichan traces the history of women's access to the law profession, in *Les Québécoises et le barreau: L'histoire d'une difficile conquête, 1914–1941* (Sillery: Septentrion, 1999).

FOUR: WINNING THE PROVINCIAL FRANCHISE

On the Montreal Trades and Labor Council and its support for the women's vote, see Jacques Rouillard, *Aux origines de la social-démocratie québécoise: Le Conseil des métiers et du travail de Montréal (1897–1930)* (Montreal: M Éditeur, 2018). Maryse Darsigny relates the history of the League for Women's Rights in her master's thesis, which is cited in the section for Chapter 3. For the Canadian Alliance for Women's Vote in Quebec, see Diane Lamoureux, *Citoyennes? Femmes, droit de vote et démocratie* (Montreal: Éditions du remue-ménage, 1989).

Aline Charles discusses the conception of citizenship of women who demanded an old-age pension from the Taschereau government, in "Femmes âgées, pauvres et sans droit de vote, mais … citoyennes? Lettres au premier ministre du Québec, 1935–1936," *Recherches féministes* 26, 2 (2013): 51–70. The brief presented by the League for Women's Rights to the Rowell-Sirois Commission is in Micheline Dumont and Louise Toupin, *La pensée féministe au Québec: Anthologie [1900–1985]* (Montreal: Éditions du remue-ménage, 2003). For Casgrain's thought and her position with regard to feminism and nationalism, see Nicole Forget, *Thérèse Casgrain: La gauchiste en collier de perles* (Montreal: Fides, 2013); Susan Mann Trofimenkoff, "Thérèse Casgrain and the CCF in Quebec," in *Beyond the Vote: Canadian Women and Politics*, ed. Linda Kealey and Joan Sangster (Toronto: University of Toronto Press, 1989), 139–68; and Maryse Darsigny, "La 'femme moderne' selon Thérèse Casgrain: une analyse de son discours féministe des années trente," in *Thérèse Casgrain: Une femme tenace et engagée*, ed. Anita Caron and Lorraine Archambault (Sainte-Foy: Presses de l'Université du Québec, 1993), 119–38. On the first orientation meeting of the Quebec Liberal Party, see Jacques Rouillard, "Aux sources de la Révolution tranquille: le congrès d'orientation du Parti libéral du Québec du 10 et 11 juin 1938," *Bulletin d'histoire politique* 24, 1 (2015): 125–58.

On the struggle of English Canadian feminists to get women recognized as persons and thus eligible for appointment to the senate, see Robert J. Sharpe and Patricia I. McMahon, *The Persons Case: The Origins and Legacy of the Fight for Legal Personhood* (Toronto: Osgoode Society for Canadian Legal History and University of Toronto Press, 2007). For the demands of Quebec feminists regarding civil rights, see Jennifer Stoddart, "Quand des gens de robe se penchent sur les droits des femmes: le cas de la commission Dorion, 1929–1931," in *Travailleuses et féministes: Les femmes dans la société québécoise*, ed. Marie Lavigne and Yolande Pinard (Montreal: Boréal express, 1983), 307–35.

Finally, for an analysis of the causes of the delay in the enfranchisement of Quebec women, see Sylvie D'Augerot-Arend, "Why So Late? Cultural and Institutional Factors in the Granting of Quebec and French Women's Political Rights," *Revue d'études canadiennes/Journal of Canadian Studies* 26, 1 (1991): 138–65; and Alexandre

Dumas, "Le droit de vote des femmes à l'Assemblée législative du Québec (1922–1940)," *Bulletin d'histoire politique* 24, 3 (2016): 137–57.

FIVE: REACHING FOR REPRESENTATION

Concerning Indigenous peoples and the vote, see Richard H. Bartlett, "Citizens Minus: Indians and the Right to Vote," *Saskatchewan Law Review* 44 (1979–80): 163–94; Lesley A. Jacobs, "Mapping the Legal Consciousness of First Nations Voters: Understanding Voting Rights Mobilization" (paper presented at the Aboriginal Policy Research Conference, Ottawa, 9–12 March 2009); and Daniel Guérin, "La participation des Autochtones aux élections fédérales canadiennes: tendances et conséquences," in "Les Autochtones et les élections," special issue, *Perspectives électorales* 5, 3 (2003): 11–17.

On Indigenous women's participation in the governance of their communities, see Mélissa Guillemette, "Gouvernance autochtone: retrouver l'équilibre," *La Gazette des femmes*, 6 February 2015, https://www.gazettedesfemmes.ca/11077/gouvernance-autochtone-retrouver-lequilibre/; and Anny Morissette, "Composer avec un système imposé: La tradition et le conseil de bande à Manawan," *Recherches amérindiennes au Québec* 37, 2–3 (2007): 127–38.

For Indigenous women's demands concerning the Indian Act, see, in particular, Wayne Brown, "Mary-Two-Axe Earley: militante des droits à l'égalité des femmes autochtones," in "Les Autochtones et les élections," special issue, *Perspectives électorales* 5, 3 (2003): 58–62; and Amanda Ricci, "Bâtir une communauté citoyenne: Le militantisme chez les femmes autochtones pendant les années 1960 à 1990," *Recherches amérindiennes au Québec* 46, 1 (2016): 75–85. Regarding violence on reserves, see Lyse Montminy, Renée Brassard, Mylène Jaccoud, Elizabeth Harper, Marie-Pierre Bousquet, and Shanie Leroux, "Pour une meilleure compréhension des particularités de la violence familiale vécue par les femmes autochtones au Canada," *Nouvelles pratiques sociales* 23, 1 (2010): 53–66. On gender relations in Indigenous communities, notably that of the Mohawks, see Patricia Monture-Angus, *Thunder in My Soul: A Mohawk Woman Speaks* (Halifax: Fernwood, 1995). Audra Simpson also addresses this subject in *Mohawk Interruptus: Political Life across the Borders of Settler States* (Durham, NC: Duke University Press, 2014). She examines the Mohawk refusal to recognize the legitimacy of the white government.

To understand the events around the Oka crisis, see Geoffrey York and Loreen Pindera, *People of the Pines: The Warriors and the Legacy of Oka* (Boston: Little, Brown, 1991). On the place of Indigenous women in the economic development of northern Quebec, see Michelle Audette, "Les femmes ont-elles une place dans le Plan Nord," and Évelyne Roy, "Le Plan Nord québécois: Quelle place pour les femmes autochtones?" in "Les peuples Autochtones et le Plan Nord: éléments pour un débat," ed. Carole Lévesque, Daniel Salée, and Iona Radu, *Cahiers DIALOG* 4 (2012): 35–36 and 37–48.

On the question of women's place in partisan politics, see Manon Tremblay, *Québécoises et représentation parlementaire* (Quebec City: Presses de l'Université Laval, 2005); and Monique Michaud, "Les candidatures féminines aux élections québécoises: d'hier à aujourd'hui," *Bulletin Bibliothèque de l'Assemblée nationale* 39, 1 (2010): 30–33.

For more on the content of the *Manifeste pour un Québec solidaire* and the *Manifeste pour un Québec lucide*, see, respectively, http://jmt-sociologue.uqac.ca/www/word/387_135_CH/lecon_3/pourunquebecsolidaire.pdf and http://classiques.uqac.ca/contemporains/finances_publiques_qc/manifeste_qc_lucide.pdf.

With regard to the results of the 1 October 2018 provincial election, see Jessica Nadeau, "Le Parlement atteindra la zone de parité," *Le Devoir*, 2 October 2018.

To find out more about the debates concerning parity, see Chantal Maillé, "Depuis cinquante ans à l'Assemblée nationale mais toujours loin de la parité," in "Les femmes en politique québécoise depuis 50 ans," special issue, *Bulletin d'histoire politique* 20, 2 (2011): 80–92; Pascale Navarro, *Femmes et pouvoir: Les changements nécessaires: Plaidoyer pour la parité* (Montreal: Léméac, 2015); Joan Wallach Scott, *Parité! Sexual Equality and the Crisis of French Universalism* (Chicago: University of Chicago Press, 2005); and Eleni Varikas, "Une représentation en tant que femme? Réflexions critiques sur la demande de la parité des sexes," *Nouvelles questions féministes* 16, 2 (1995): 81–127.

On women parliamentarians and parity, see the article by Jocelyne Richer of Canadian Press, "Parité homme-femme à l'Assemblée nationale: D'ex-élues réclament une loi," reproduced in *Metro*, 5 March 2017 (http://journalmetro.com/actualites/national/1098928/parite-dex-elues-reclament-une-loi/).

The question of relations between women and civil rights in Quebec is addressed in Marie-Laurence Beaumier, "Le genre et les limites de l'Universalité: La Ligue des Droits de l'Homme du Québec, 1963–1985" (master's thesis, Université Laval, 2012); and Dominique Clément, *Canada's Rights Revolution: Social Movements and Social Change, 1937–82* (Vancouver: UBC Press, 2008).

The report of the Bouchard-Taylor commission can be read at https://www.mce.gouv.qc.ca/publications/CCPARDC/rapport-final-integral-en.pdf (in French: https://www.mce.gouv.qc.ca/publications/CCPARDC/rapport-final-integral-fr.pdf).

The connections between feminism and nationalism are examined in Diane Lamoureux, *L'amère patrie: Féminisme et nationalisme dans le Québec contemporain* (Montreal: Éditions du remue-ménage, 2001). For the feminism of elected representatives, see Micheline Dumont, "Politique active et féminisme: Les députées de l'Assemblée nationale," in "Les femmes en politique québécoise depuis 50 ans," special issue, *Bulletin d'histoire politique* 20, 2 (2011): 46–60. Dumont discusses the impact of the Yvettes incident, in "Les Yvettes ont permis aux femmes d'entrer dans l'histoire politique," *L'Action nationale* 80, 8 (1990): 1041–45. Stéphanie Godin also studies this subject, in "Les Yvettes comme l'expression d'un féminisme fédéraliste au Québec," *Mens: revue d'histoire intellectuelle de l'Amérique française* 5, 1 (2004): 73–117. Finally, on the question of women's real power in politics, see Lise Payette, *Le pouvoir? Connais pas!* (Montreal: Québec/Amérique, 1981).

PHOTO CREDITS

Page 3:   Drawing by Bernard Duchesne.

Page 31:   "Votes for Women," *Montreal Herald,* 26 November 1913, courtesy of *Montreal Gazette.*

Page 34:   Ladies Benevolent Institution, Montreal, 1909, McCord Museum, II-174471.

Page 39:   *Filles de la Sagesse à l'hôpital Sainte-Justine,* 1910. Photograph from Archives historiques du CHU Sainte-Justine, Montréal, Québec, Canada.

Page 63:   "Les suffragettes à Montréal," *Le Canard,* 23 April 1911, 1, Bibliothèque et Archives nationales du Québec, JOU 1545 CON.

Page 77:   "Quand maman votera," *Almanach de la langue française,* 1929, Bibliothèque et Archives nationales du Québec, PER Z-919.

Page 82:   Idola Saint-Jean, Antoinette Mercure, and Nora Sampson, late 1920s, Alain Gariépy Collection, Assemblée nationale du Québec.

Page 97:   "Women Brave Cold Seeking Vote," *Montreal Daily Star,* 16 December 1929, courtesy of *Montreal Gazette,* Bibliothèque et Archives nationales du Québec, JOU 1038 CON.

Page 103:   "Please Let Mummy Vote," League for Women's Rights poster, 1930s. Archives de la Ville de Montréal, BM014-4_02 op.

Page 123:   Civil Code as an old man, *Montreal Herald,* 22 November 1929, courtesy of *Montreal Gazette.*

Page 126:   "Progressive Turkey," *Montreal Daily Star,* 8 February 1935, Assemblée nationale du Québec archives.

Page 127:   Jacques Gagnier, "Laquelle préférez-vous?" *Quartier Latin,* 10 November 1939, courtesy of Francine Gagnier and family.

Page 132:   "Really, This Is So Sudden," *Toronto Star,* 25 April 1940.

Page 135:   *Monument en hommage aux femmes en politique,* 2012, sculpture by Jules Lasalle, photo by Francois Laliberté, Assemblée nationale du Québec archives.

Page 142: Mary Two-Axe Earley, 1983, Harold Rosenburg/*Toronto Star.*

Page 149: "Women Exercise Franchise for First Time," *Montreal Gazette,* 9 August 1944, 4, Bibliothèque et Archives nationales du Québec, JOU 409 CON.

Page 150: Election poster for Idola Saint-Jean, 1930, Archives de la Ville de Montréal, BM102_140p.

Page 152: Marie-Claire Kirkland-Casgrain with politicians, Quebec Liberal Party archives.

Page 154: Thérèse Casgrain campaigning for election, 1958 [1953?], Canadian Press, photo 8968027.

INDEX

O'Connor, Mae Leehy, 151
office, women candidates for. *See*
political candidates, women as
Oka crisis (1990), 146
Ontario and female suffrage, 64–66
Option citoyenne movement, 156
Ottawa, Éva, 139–40

Pachano, Violet, 139
Pankhurst, Emmeline, 67
Papineau, Louis-Joseph, 15–16, 17, 75
Paquet, Louis-Adolphe, Monsignor, 76
Parent, Sylvie, 158
Parité! (Scott), 161
Parker Drummond, Julia. *See*
Drummond, Julia Parker
Parti canadien. *See* Parti patriote
Parti patriote (*formerly* Parti canadien):
contested election in William-Henry
riding, 11; on dower, 26–27; favoured
by women, 9, 14; Montreal West by-
election (1832) and its impact, 12–14,
16–18; newspaper's printing petition supporting property as basis for
vote, 10; supported women's vote, 11.
See also Patriotes (in rebellions of
1837–38)
Parti québécois: Bill 60, Quebec Charter
of Values, 167–68; cabinet of René
Lévesque, 165; new Quebec nationalism, 170–71; secularism, 167–68;
women candidates, 152
Parti social démocratique, 152, 154
patriarchy: citizenship perceived as
male, 14, 15, 17; in colonial era, 4–5;
colonizers' norm imposed in Indigenous peoples, 138; female suffrage a
challenge to, x–xi, xiii, 77–78, 95, 108,
129–30; male vote the "legitimate"
vote, 13; opposition to suffragists,
x–xi; suffrage threat to gender identity, 108, 129–30, 133; women's role,

xi, 28–29 (*see also* gender; separate
spheres)
Patriotes (in rebellions of 1837–38), 20–
22, 25. *See also* rebellions of 1837–38
Payette, Lise, 165, 169–71
Pelletier, Louis, 60, 68
Pelletier, Toussaint, 21
periodicals. *See* media
Perrault, Marie-Claire, 16–17
Perrin, M.-L., Father, 79, 87, 91
physicians, female. *See* professions,
access to
Picard, Ghislain, 145
Picard, Nathalie, 8–9, 10, 14
Pius XI, Pope, 91
Plamondon, Édith, 106
Le Plan Nord, 146–47
Plante, Anatole, 118(t), 121, 124, 125
Plante, Valérie, 158
political candidates, women as: candidacy gender quotas, 159–62; federal
candidates (1940s and 1950s), 149–
51; obstacles to running, 148–49,
158–59, 174; provincial candidates,
percentages, 154, 159, 160; replacing
deceased male relative, 152; Thérèse
Casgrain's runs for office, 84–85
political office, women in: difference vs
equality of sexes, 161–62; distancing
from feminism, 168–69, 174–75;
federal, 150–51; feminist commitment, 168–69; gender parity and
democratic deficit, 160; ministers
and party leaders, 163–65, 169; municipal, 156–58; numbers, 158, 174;
provincial, 136, 151–52, 154, 158, 169;
question of democratic deficit, 160
political parties: CCF (Co-operative
Commonwealth Federation), 84–85,
152; Coalition avenir Québec, 169;
Conservative Party of Canada, 70–71,
73, 74–78; Labor-Progressive Party,

province, 109; photograph, 82; quotes in *Montreal Herald*, 96; racist argument for suffrage, 125, 126(i); radio talks on female suffrage and citizenship rights, 100, 108, 119; on role of MLAs in history of suffrage, vii; speech supporting female suffrage in Legislative Assembly (1922), 82, 83–84; on UN Universal Declaration of Human Rights, viii; on women's interest in social legislation, 121–22; women's right to access job market, 104–6. *See also* Canadian Alliance for Women's Vote in Quebec (CAWVQ)

Saint-Michel, Julien. *See* Circé-Côté, Éva

Sampson, Nora, 82(i), 101

Saskatchewan and Asian Canadians' vote, 136

Sauvé, Jeanne, 150–51

school board appointments, Montreal, 49–50

Scott, Isabella, 98, 122

Scott, Joan, 161

Seguin, Renaud, 9

Sénécal, Marie Louise, 57

separate spheres: belief in complementarity between sexes, 40–41; conservative nationalist view, 74–75, 94–95; description, xii–xiii; gender roles according to Custom of Paris, 4–5; ideology hindered female franchise, 32; "legitimate" voter male, 13; loss of vote, women's indifference to (1834 or 1849), 19–20, 32; maternalistic argument re porous border between spheres, xiii; no longer existing (1930s), 121; Patriotes' beliefs (during rebellions), 25; reasoning in denying women the vote, 55–59, 61, 75–77; suffrage threat to gender identity, 108, 129–30, 133; women's

duties domestic and maternal, 14–15, 28–29, 74–76, 94; women's political participation "unnatural," 14–15, 75; women's role in society, x–xi, xii–xiii, 5, 12, 14–15, 19–20, 28–29

Sertillanges, Antonin-Gilbert, Father, 126

Shadd Cary, Mary Ann, 64–65

Sherbrooke's charitable organizations, 32–33

Sicotte, Anne-Marie, 46, 73, 80, 89–90

Simpson, Audra, 143

social class: differences between labour movement and feminists, 100–1; middle class and interest in politics, 32; middle-class origins of suffragists, 90. *See also* upper-class women; working-class women

social reform: beneficial for society, 121–22; justification of demands, 40; on vote crucial to obtaining reforms, 40, 66, 84–85, 106, 173

Springtime of the People in Europe (1848), 18

Stanton-Jean, Michèle, 101

Stewart, Andrew, 10

Stuart, James, 11

study clubs and literary societies, 32, 65

suffrage movement: arguments for suffrage in 1930s, 114–16; citizenship and, 13–15, 55; ethnicity, class, racism, and motivation, xiv–xv; fragmentation before First World War, 68–69; lack of militancy, xi–xii, 97; Legislative Assembly presentations (1922), 64, 80–86; Legislative Assembly presentations (1927–1940), 116–17, 118(t), 119–20, 131; maternalistic and egalitarian arguments, xii–xiii, 82–83, 173; Ontario's fight for suffrage, 64–66; origins (*see* women's movement, 1880s to early 1900s);

Printed and bound in Canada by Friesens
Set in Gill Sans and Tundra by Artegraphica Design Co. Ltd.
Copy editor: Deborah Kerr
Proofreader: Kristy Lynn Hankewitz
Indexer: Patricia Buchanan
Cover designer: Jessica Sullivan